GOOD LADS PLAY FOOTBALL

A YEAR VISIT AT THE CHELSEA AND ARSENAL ACADEMIES

GOOD LADS PLAY FOOTBALL

A YEAR VISIT AT THE CHELSEA AND ARSENAL ACADEMIES

Shlomit Guy

First published in Great Britain in 2015 by DB Publishing, an imprint of
JMD Media Ltd

ISBN 978-1-78091-531-9

Printed and bound in the UK by Copytech (UK) Ltd Peterborough

Contents

Prologue

Heathrow

Thursday, at midnight, in the arrivals terminal at Heathrow Airport. I'm waiting at the baggage claim with dozens of tourists from Italy, who came with me on the same flight. Large bags pass in front of my exhausted face. I was tired from the long journey and the long wait I had in Milan for the connecting flight, which I chose in order to save some travel costs. Twenty minutes past twelve, I can tell how time passes by the rate of incoming luggage. A big one, and thirty seconds later, comes a small one. The third one marks a minutes passing. The large cool hall begins to empty of people. Suitcases on the conveyor become sparse, and the time that elapses between one to the next lengthens. Only the new big bag that I bought specifically for this trip has not appeared among the long leather straps that mark the end of the journey. Ten more minutes pass. I am left alone in the hall. The flight has been already replaced on the screen. And I, though no longer a little girl, feel like a lost baby. This is the first time I have travelled alone abroad, and what exactly am I supposed to do now?

Minus my suitcase I go to the clerk who's deep in an absorbing conversation with one of her colleagues, both dressed in their land steward's uniform.

"Excuse me... sorry, but my suitcase.... I just landed with a flight... not here, sorry..."

She did not even give me half a look, but with a practiced finger that knows how to recognize lost tourists, points towards the reception desk. Half past midnight. A nice guy is sitting at the Alitalia reception desk. Armed with my basic English and exhausted from too many sleepless hours, I try to explain myself.

"I came to from? Tel Aviv, now. That's… from Milan, but first Tel Aviv. And my suitcase... well, it's not here. Maybe you know…?"

The receptionist, pleasant and business like, returned with me to the conveyor. After another long wait, he comes back with the somewhat vague answer: "Well, it seems you are quite right".

But as this is my first time in England, actually the first time I ever met with a real authentic English speaking person, not through the TV screen, and I do not really understand the meaning of 'quite right'. Because where I come from there are only two possible answers to the question of whether I'm right or not. The first, which I preferred, is that I am not right. My location is about as miserable as my English, and that now I was looking for my suitcase on the wrong conveyor belt. If you kindly retrieve it for me, I promise we will part as friends. A quick computer check reveals that I was not only 'quite right' but even very right. Although I did not have the opportunity to spend more than a few minutes in Milan sadly, because after all, who wouldn't be delighted to spend a weekend of celebration in a city where one of its football teams had just reached the semi-finals of the Champions League the night before?

My suitcase, however, did win the dubious pleasure and remain in a pool of lost luggage, along with some other ridiculously expensive Italian handbags. And this way – the first time I dare to poke my nose out from the embracing and protecting borders of Israel, at the ripe old age of twenty-seven, I suddenly discovers what helplessness means, and there is not even a black suitcase beside me to pull out a tissue from to wipe away my tears.

One AM. Not the best time to lose your senses. The nice clerk asks for the address where I'll be staying.

"Your suitcase will arrive at that address no later than three pm tomorrow," he promises. I open a little notebook and copy the address of Johnny, a friend of a friend from back home, onto a stack of papers. Johnny agreed to accommodate me for my first three days in London, despite the fact we've never met before. My delay due to my suitcase drama makes me think how long he will be willing to wait for a complete stranger. After leaving the cursed Alitalia desk, I try calling Johnny on my Israeli cell phone. 01244... I punch in the number I remember from my previous Israel to England overseas phone calls. An error dial tone greets my ear. I try again. 01244... And again the same tone. What's going on? Don't panic, I tell myself. I was responsible enough to leave the number with my parents in Israel. I decide to call my mom and make sure I didn't miss a digit. It's about three in the morning back home but hey… it's not too early here either. First the dialling code, then the country code, then region and then my parents house familiar number. My fingers fly across the keypad with confidence 0129728… Again the same three long circular cocky tones, I try to keep cool in spite of my hidden despair. I try again but again. No success. I'm only four hours away from home but I feel like I'm on a different planet.

In my despair I sit on a small bench outside the by now nearly empty airport. My two carry-on handbags stand still beside me. I don't know whether to take a taxi to my destination address, or to go on trusting this small bench that looked a little safer. Another shot on the cell phone yields the same frustrating outcome. For centuries, researchers have been travelling to the farthest corners of the world, and somehow manage to communicate with the natives in extinct languages. And here I am, in one of the most advanced cities in the world, can't even make a local phone call. Two challenging years in the Israeli army and seven long academic years haven't prepared me for this.

A cool April breeze awakes me from my reverie, reminding me that my coat is, where else, buried deep in my suitcase. It's around three thirty am in Israel. In about four hours my mother is going to wake up from her deep sleep and start cooking for the Sabbath. Weekend papers will be waiting at the front door of each house; housewives will hurry around markets with their last minute shopping. Here, it feels like no one really cares, not about the Sabbath, not about my suitcase nor about yours truly. I fiddle around with my cell phone, the only light source around. Suddenly, a text message that I received a couple hours ago, during the flight, appears. A spark of optimism manages to penetrate through the cold apathetic atmosphere; someone is thinking about me. A higher force sent someone who can help me.

"Maccabi Tel-Aviv have lost to CSKA 92-77, there goes the final four", was written in the text message that was sent by my friend Shimi, whose friend Johnny was waiting for me in a far corner of the city at this very moment. With all due respect and sympathy to the disappointed basketball supporters from Tel Aviv, I hit the green 'send' button. Shimi answers with a sleepy voice. He doesn't really understand what I want, but he can hear me crying. After some calming efforts at his side and some explanations from my side, he promises me he will take care of this mess.

"And you, stay exactly where you are," he orders, as if there was somewhere else for me to go.

Forty minutes later I pay a taxi driver the obscene amount of sixty pounds, a sum that could buy me a pampering weekend in Israel. A sleepy figure emerges for the building, wearing pyjamas; Johnny. I give him a warm hug of gratitude, one that only someone who minutes ago was sure she was going to spend the next couple of nights arguing over public benches, with random homeless people, can give. Only when he asks me if I need help with my luggage I almost lose my peace again.

London

My first morning in London and I am pretty drowsy. I wake up late, snuggling in the warm bed of Johnny's guest room. My suitcase is supposed to arrive sometime this afternoon but so far I have received no text message regarding its arrival. I hope it arrives sooner rather than later, as my battery is running low, and the charger is, where else, but in the suitcase. Johnny leaves to go to work as a bartender in a small café in Piccadilly Circus, leaving me with his three English cats, who seems to be as sleepy as I am. I follow my morning ritual and automatically turn on the radio. Fast murmurs emerge from the speakers; I can barely make any sense of it. Something makes the reporter laugh. British humour of some sort that I can't begin to understand. It doesn't take me to long to abandon my intellectual morning ritual. I have three phone numbers in my blue notebook that I need to use by the end of the day. All three belong to the heads of large football academies. I still have a couple of hours until my deadline to make the dreaded calls, according to Arik's instructions. These three calls will determine my future in the big city. Without being too dramatic, these three calls will probably determine the rest of my life.

Less than six months ago, I submitted my Masters project to Ben Gurion University of the Negev. What would someone that has just finished a big, exhausting project like to do next? Take time off? Travel? Or alternatively, start thinking about his or her PhD research project? Yes, that's me. The subject of the research was no brainer; football will obviously be the main subject. The social and cultural life that developed around it totally represented a profound social process in English society and seemed intriguing to me. Excitement and passion surrounds what was once a working class sport, drawing more and more attention from researchers from a variety of areas.

England has always fascinated me. I cannot put my finger on the exact reason but England always seemed to be a distant, mysterious and unreachable place. I felt somewhat nostalgic towards it, though any connection between the royal family and me will be purely coincidental. English football has a magic about it that I couldn't explain. The dramatic change it had undergone, from a working class sport and as such: violent, male-dominated and threatening, to what it is today: an almost noble branch of sport, aesthetic and almost aristocratic, ignited my imagination. I am familiar with the popular claims about the police and court system's role in taming the game of football, but I could never bring myself to believe that it was Mrs Thatcher's harsh policy that terrified thousands of hooligans, who were a common sight in football stadiums during those days, and was responsible for the revolution. That is what I wanted to investigate.

Four years is the time period that it usually takes to complete a Ph.D. research in Israel's academy. During this time I wanted to learn as much as I could about England and its football. But where do I start? England is huge, both in size and population, especially to someone coming from a remote spot in the Middle East. Football in England is played on every available patch of grass and street corner. When I started thinking about the first steps of my research, Football academies were the first thing that crossed my mind. These institutions are educational systems where talented young lads, with potential to be professional football players come to in order to get a proper football education. One could learn about the values and norms that are expected from a first class Football player in these institutions. Educational institutions are generally places of 'ideal' social life. Elementary school, for example, is where, alongside with learning basic technical and functional skills, children are taught values such as patriotism, social justice, self-accomplishment etc. In other words, the children learn what is important in the eyes of society and how one should behave.

Therefore, football academies are the perfect place to examine the model concept that English football has been trying to create since the 1990s. It is very likely that along with functional training, the academies will instil the values and the norms that are expected of an English football player. Understanding those expectations is a big step on the way to understanding English football as a whole. Once my mission was clear and the goal was set, it was only a matter of getting research approval from one of the academies in England. The practical task, however, turned out to be the hardest. My plan was to send a few requests to a number of academies in England (today every club in the top three leagues has one), get their approval, pack my bags and travel westward. The email and the Internet turned out to be quite useful in finding contacts in the football academies, so I sent my resume along with a formal letter to a couple dozens of them. Reply letters started to arrive one after the other; as polite and courteous as they were disappointing. In retrospect it turns out that they receive dozens of letters like mine every day from every corner in the world. They are all answered automatically, in the same polite, very English manner. I have to admit, my request was pretty bold... English football is such a huge sensation, I should know. Only few outstanding people get to receive a warm welcome there. And I was asking to get access to spend a full year with these wonder boys whom, who knows what their price tag will be tomorrow...

"What do you need so much time for?" the immigrations clerk in Tel Aviv embassy asked in wonderment. Suddenly my dream regarding English football seemed unreachable. Too bad, I had so many great ideas...

Aside from my broken heart, time was running out. It has been three months since I was accepted this Ph.D. programme, and I was supposed to submit my research proposal in nine months, including details regarding the research ideas and location. I couldn't think of a way to get where I want. The frustration was beginning to creep in. Instead of dealing with understanding the English football, I had to figure a way how to get closer to English football. I didn't expect this. This is it, my last round of calls, I promised myself. If this fails, I'll stay in Israel to investigate local football.

I had to have a Plan B. So I though, in my hometown, I know some people who know some people who could help. I know, 'people who know people' is such an Israeli way to work, but with no other alternative I had to

(I guess I could) use my Israeli skills (in such a case). I set an appointment with Vikko Haddad, a highly respected local trainer. I wasn't expecting much from the meeting and I was already in the late stages of despair as to the future of this project. Vikko, however, sounded thrilled about the idea, and introduced me to Amnon Raz from the Israeli Football Association (IFA) who has been working on Israeli projects related to English football. I tried to keep my expectations low here as well. Amnon listened very patiently and then said: "We have a guy in London. His name is Arik. Write down his number".

Arik Yahalomi is the association's non-official contact in London. At this stage I'm not really sure where I'm heading, but I feel I'm making some progress. Arik answers the phone. He has already spoken to Amnon and heard about my project. He asks me to tell him a little more about my plan but at this stage I'm not sure what more can I tell.

"Listen, young lady," he gently admonishes me, "England is not Israel, and sentences like 'I don't really know' do not work here. I can try to help you, but I'm asking of you, next time we talk, you have to know exactly what you're going to ask, these are managers of the biggest clubs in the world".

I get a bit frightened, but I give him my word.

Our next conversation took place in a little coffee shop in Tel Aviv, during one of his vacations in Israel. Arik was fully attentive this time. After I finished talking, he pulled out a big envelope and handed me phone numbers of three academy heads in London, three detailed maps, detailing the public transport that I will need to take on my way to my first three meetings at Arsenal, Chelsea and Queens Park Rangers (QPR) academies. He had already spoken with them. Now I need to call them to schedule a time and date.

"You shouldn't have any problems", Arik assures me, and wishes me luck.

That's it. Three weeks later I find myself in a small apartment on Victoria Street, having so far meet only the Alitalia receptionist, Johnny and three local cats that needed to be fed. The airline company hasn't called about my suitcase yet but something else is really getting my blood pumping. In a moment, when the clock hits two pm, lunchtime at the academies, I am supposed to call the heads and set a date for an appointment.

I have memorized my speech: "hello, my name is Shlomit, I am a friend of Arik's from the Israeli Football Association and I would really appreciate if you could meet me for a short talk". At the moment of truth I get over my fear and embarrassment, and hit the dial button. No answer at the Chelsea Academy. Nor at Queens Park Rangers either.

"Arsenal Academy," a voice replies after the second ring. Mr Smith, the acting director of the academy, is a warm-hearted person.

"Of course we can meet," he agrees. "When will be a convenient time for you? Do you know the way? If there is any problem, please feel free to call again".

The call flew smoothly. A couple minutes later I thank him and hang up. I take a minute to look in the mirror. A pale, shaky figure is looking back at me. I don't give it much thought, I scheduled my first meeting!

Academy Visits

This book is the fruit of my research regarding English football, during the 2007/08 season. My research truly began when I got the approval from the Arsenal and Chelsea academy heads to conduct my research in their facilities. It was a little harder to reach the Chelsea academy head, as he was on an educational tour in Italy, when I tried to reach him. Upon his return we met at the academy's training facility in Cobham, a small town about thirty kilometres southwest of London. After I reassured him that I wouldn't use the information I receive in an improper manner, he gave me a green light to start my research at the academy. I also met the Queens Park Rangers academy head at that time and I intended to include his academy in my research. Sudden changes in the academy, including changes in management, as well as practical difficulties to reach this distant location, made me forgo my research there and focus on Arsenal and Chelsea. In the following months I visited the Arsenal and Chelsea academies, once or twice a week, attended practices of all ages, watched friendly matches with fellow academies and participated in frontal theoretical classes given to these children. I also interviewed the managers, talked to coaches, and even took the time to talk unofficially with some of these young players' parents.

It was a wonderful beginning which taught me plenty about the ideal English football player model, which the academies and Premier League wished to create. Later on, I was exposed to the various activities that the football clubs initiated for the welfare of their communities. I interviewed the head of the Arsenal Community department, he told me about the local, national and international activities. In my journey to understand the change in English football, I attended dozens of matches of the three main Leagues and interviewed the players and coaches. It was clear that the transformation in football's social status affected not only the academies, but also the professional Leagues. I toured the stadiums and visited the clubs' official museums. These museums, which were recently built by some of the Premier League clubs, aim to tell a story far beyond the clubs' objective story. Museums in general are means of displaying a cultural peak. The football club museums aim to include English football as an integral part of England social and cultural legacy.

This book tells the story of my research experience and demonstrates some of the ideas I had during my journey. This is my personal experience in England; it could be, and probably is, different from the experience other people who lived there at the same time I was. One can compare this book to an impressionistic painting; unlike the realistic artist's goal, to transfer a lively three dimensional image to a two dimensional canvas, the impressionistic artist wishes to express his impression of reality as he sees it through his eyes. This book shares my experience and conclusions from the events during the 2007/08 football season.

Most of the peoples' names mentioned in this book have been changed in order to protect their privacy. Personal information and certain incidents were altered to avoid possible recognition. This mainly refers to the children in the academy. The people who are introduced by their full names have either totally agreed, or information concerning them was obtained from the mass media.

In order not to put the royal cart before its magnificent royal horses, we shall return to the afternoon hour, in the middle of April of 2007. I am still in a little apartment on Victoria Street, standing in front of my pale reflection, just after a successful conversation with the Arsenal academy head. We still have a long way ahead of us. In hindsight, it was worth every second.

Johnny

Johnny is a diehard Arsenal fan. When he gets back from work, around 3 pm, I tell him enthusiastically about the significant progress I made today. He is happy for me, but within minutes he falls asleep on the couch, next to his three cats, which so far did nothing but eat lunch and nap all day.

"I had a long day", Johnny apologises.

As a matter of fact he did not get any sleep last night, but Johnny is a typical Englishman; he will never say, or even hint something that would make you feel unwelcome, no matter how late you showed up. I was tired of wallowing in this common litter box, so I decide to go out and conquer the big city. Well, maybe not conquer, but at least to get acquainted with one of London's best-known facilities – the Tube. I get dressed in my not too good smelling clothes from yesterday, seeing that my suitcase, how surprising, hasn't arrived yet, and leave. I set off to meet Guy, Arik's friend at a completely unfamiliar train station named Swiss Cottage. He is supposed to give me two tickets to the Arsenal match this weekend, one for me and one for my generous host.

As it turns out, Victoria station is the wrong place to have my first formal introduction with English society. It's rush hour, thousands of people, hurrying home from work pass by me. This is the place of departure for trains crossing all over London, England and Europe. I stare at the Tube's map and play an imaginary 'Snakes and Ladders' with myself; I need to get on a train here and change at Green Park in order to get to Swiss Cottage Station on the northwest side of the city. I walk over to the ticket booth to buy a ticket with a much bigger note than I needed, I haven't figured out the coin system yet. With the self-confidence of someone who has just accomplished her first mission, I step onto the escalators heading down to the underground. My head aimed forward and my eyes searching for directional signs. Suddenly, I feel someone breathing down my neck. "Excuse me", I turn around. A young man in a suit and tie carrying a James Bond briefcase looks at me with eyes full of despair. He looks like he's in a hurry, and I don't quite understand why he had just stopped behind me. Another second of bewilderment passes and I move aside to the right of the escalators, to let him pass. I asked myself why didn't the young guy just go around me, and suddenly realize that all the standing people are on the right side of the escalators, while all the hurrying people, fly by on the left. It seems so clear and simple now, I just can't believe I didn't see it earlier. I take a moment to get embarrassed by my rookie mistake. A moment later I go on the next escalator and stand on its right side along with the rest of the people, it feels great.

I manage to find the right station and meet Guy. We chat for a bit about English football and academic stuff, he hands me the tickets and I hurry back to Victoria Station This time I make no mistakes; I stand on the right side of the escalator, I switch trains and step out of the station just as the sun is setting over the city. Dozens of sophisticated looking youngsters fill the local bars with glasses in their hands, enjoying the beginning of the weekend. Back at the apartment, Johnny asks if I want to go out for a drink. I do. While getting ready I scan through my day's achievements. Although I still don't have my suitcase and my phone is threatening to die, I got two tickets to the Arsenal versus Bolton match on Saturday and an arranged meeting with an academy head. I also have a couple of hours' worth of Tube experience, which I obtained all by myself. I feel good.

April 2007: Johnny's Arsenal, Arsenal's Johnny

Arsenal

Johnny was born into a family of Arsenal supporters, and spent his weekends as a boy at the Highbury football stadium, back when tickets cost only a couple of pounds. His mother was born in Israel to a poor immigrant family from Yemen. She came on a trip to London over forty years ago, that's when she met her future husband. Johnny's father is a Jewish Englishman, who drives a black taxi for a living. His mother use to work as a peddler in the tourist areas until recently. They live in a small house with a small yard and a dog in north London, barely making a living. All the more so since Johnny's elderly mother had stopped working due to the arduous nature of her job. Johnny had left the house a couple of years ago and lived in rented apartments ever since. His job as a barista in a small coffee shop in the city centre barely pays his bills. Tickets to Arsenal matches are, of course, out of the question. Season tickets cost as much as a month's salary, and single match tickets are nearly impossible to find. When you do find one, the price is sky high, out of reach for Johnny's current lifestyle.

He hasn't had a chance to visit the Emirates Stadium yet, so during one of our long distance London to Israel phone calls, he accepts my invitation; "Of course I'd like to join you at the match" he says excitedly. Throughout all my first night in London, visiting every possible bar in the city, Johnny couldn't stop talking about tomorrow's match.

It's Saturday morning. He got up extremely early and insisted we spend the day according to the traditional football supporters' schedule, which opens with a traditional breakfast in an authentic English café.

When anthropologists say 'authentic' they mean a real, natural and primal activity; a custom or way of life that the hands of time and modernisation did not get to change yet. The concept of 'Authenticity' in no longer popular as it used to be, because of the fact that overseas travelling and satellite TV are more common today than they used to be. The search for a primal lifestyle, that hasn't been affected by other cultures or by the changing times, is now believed to be in vain. London, as many other European capitals, attracts working immigration in growing numbers and millions of tourists per year. One of the most visible outcomes is different and varied cuisines from all around the world. Therefore, when Johnny insists that we have a traditional English breakfast in an authentic café, he is actually trying to tell a story about the English culture, about the 'real' customs of the English football supporters, as he sees them.

I let him lead the way. A good breakfast certainly won't hurt right now; two days of canned food and excessive amounts of beer are taking their toll on me. We are walking through the busy downtown streets while Johnny is busy looking for a little deli where we can have breakfast. First, he looks through the window, then he examines the display refrigerators and the menus, which are written on a small blackboard with white chalk, and only then he decides that it is not 'authentic' enough and leaves. This ceremony is repeated in the next three delis, but with no satisfaction. I'm starting to get tired but I voice no complaint. We stop by a couple more delis but each of them lacks the 'authentic' part. Time is starting to creep towards the afternoon and I start questioning the idea of getting to the stadium on time. Finally, Johnny walks into a not-so-small coffee house and decides that this is it – we found our place. We sit down and order our breakfast.

On the street-facing window there is a sign that says: 'Protect the real English café'. Johnny explains that during the last few years markets and cafés serving cheap multi-cultural food opened all across the city. Those cafés hurt the fragile cultural texture of the English breakfast, and the English identity altogether. The cry to 'Protect the real English café' is aimed at that phenomenon. While we are talking, two gigantic plates arrive at our table, each of them including two eggs, fresh mushrooms, hot beans, cooked tomatoes, sausage, bacon and French fries. The amount of food on one plate does not look edible by a single person. Only one thing is missing – the English tea. I ask Johnny about it. After clearing his throat he answers: "they charge a pound and a half for one cup of tea. The owner is aware that an English breakfast must include tea and therefore charges for it separately. I'm not willing to pay that amount. A glass of tap water will do for me". Oh well, we won't let a small detail like that ruin our 'authentic' English tradition.

It might be a little inappropriate, but I suddenly notice I converted Johnny from being my kind host into my personal informant, even without noticing; I study his behaviour and listen to every word he says. Johnny is the only Englishman I know for now and there is so much more I want to learn. So I ask, and Johnny replies patiently. I study his behaviour, automatically compare it to what I'm familiar with back home. I discover many things I didn't know about the English culture. Indirectly I learn new things I didn't know about myself and my own culture. Let's take the established pre-match ritual as an example; in Israel, I used to arrive at the stadium about an hour early, to find supporters that have been decorating the stadium from early dawn. Usually, a stranger, regardless if we have met before or not, would immediately become my best friend, and the immediate enemy of the opposing team. Here, however, an hour before the match, Johnny and I finish our breakfast and head to Victoria station. I locate a few supporters that are making their way, as we are, to the Emirates Stadium. Some of them are wearing Arsenal kits. Johnny, in his official kit, doesn't talk to them. I try to notice any kind of non-verbal interaction – a wink, a nod, a touch of any kind – but between us and the other supporters there is no communication whatsoever. Everyone is making the same journey towards the same experience, but they all experience it alone. I want to ask Johnny about what seems like a strange phenomenon in my eyes, but I can't put my thoughts into words. I guess the assumption of kinship between strangers who happen to be supporters of the same football club is not as obvious as I thought to begin with. When we get to the Arsenal station on the Piccadilly line, most of the supporters get off the train. I start to follow them as Johnny stops me; "we're getting off at the next station," he says.

Noticing my panicked face, he quickly says: "everyone has their own way of getting to the match. Don't worry; we'll be there on time". We get off at the next station. Johnny wants to show me the merchandise store and buy himself some beers for the way. Thousands of supporters, wearing red and yellow shirts, the club's Home and Away colours, are everywhere, holding beer cans and linger out in the streets. While Johnny's beer started to get to him, we start walking toward the stadium. "You see here on the left? This is the legendary Highbury stadium. Now skyscrapers are being built on it".

This mass communal walk, in long straight line towards the stadium, while local joyful residents join us, from every street corner, is exhilarating. It has a sense of power.

From the outside, the stadium is magnificent; at first glance it resembles a big round concrete monster. Huge symbols carrying the stadiums name invoke a feeling of grandeur and admiration. Enthusiastic tourists – me included – take pictures from every possible angle, and pay close attention to the Arabic lettering decorating the stadium walls, despite the fact, that like me, they don't understand their meaning. I compare the feeling one gets from looking at the stadium, to the feeling that the monumental churches from the Middle Ages inspire, making a man feel tiny in the presence of God. In retrospect, I realise I was wrong; the feeling the supporters get upon their arrival to the stadium is the exact opposite from the feeling worshipers got when entering the church. Facing the strength and grandeur of the house of 'the Gunners', the Arsenal team nickname – the supporters' feel big and respectful and honoured. That is how Johnny and I feel in the entry hall. Johnny, a sworn Gunners supporter, during his first visit in the Emirates Stadium, and me, an Israeli student who arrived in London only thirty-six hours ago, for the first time in my life.

A quick look at the time reveals that we've entered the stadium with fifteen minutes left until kick-off, and according to Johnny, it's the perfect time. The feeling inside the stadium is like in a sterile bubble. A computerised system checks our tickets and, differently from Israel, there are no security guards to give you a body search or look through your bag. Police officers are nowhere to be seen and civilians wearing bright coloured vests are offering supporters help with finding their seats. We climb the stairs towards the top seats with hundreds of other excited supporters. Despite the excitement, order is maintained. Following the stairs there is a long queue at the snack bars. The supporters stand patiently, asking for this and that. The variety is large, but only healthy, un-fried food is offered.

Sandwiches are wrapped in clear plastic to keep from spreading smells. Johnny orders a beer for himself and mineral water for me. My water's label notifies me that this product is an exclusive brand, belonging to Arsenal FC.

There is no alcohol permitted in the stand, so Johnny drains the last of his beer and we go inside. The sight that lies before us a few steps inside the red chairs area is breath-taking. The grass is perfect and sprinklers that scatter water to every inch of it, cause it to glow even brighter. The sixty thousand red seats seem to be hugging each and every fan. The wave shaped open roof protects our heads from the raindrops and at the same time reveals a glimpse of the stars. All of the spectators are focussed exactly at the time of the match's opening whistle. At that moment, it feels like the whole world exists only inside the Emirates Stadium. A couple dozens of supporters, standing behind one of the goalposts, are chanting. They are only a few, but heard loudly all across the stand thanks to the perfect acoustics. We take our seats on soft padded chairs.

Beside me sits a young Arsenal supporter, but we don't exchange a word. Johnny doesn't greet his fellow supporters either. Behind us sits a grandfather with his grandson; throughout the match, they are the only voices heard. Our viewpoint is excellent. Despite the distance between us and the pitch, we feel like we can reach out and touch the players. There is no flag or sign that block our view and none of the people in front of us is standing. Johnny is thrilled. "Look at the pitch! We have the best pitch in the world! Look at the chairs! We have the best chairs in the world! I am so proud," he concludes.

The match's opening ceremony is a highly organised and well-produced event. A song is played in the stadium speakers and at its peak; both teams emerge onto the pitch. Supporters behind the gates keep singing for a short while after the music dies out. The songs are short but clear: "Arsenal FC, we're by far the greatest team the world has ever seen"; "Arsenal, Arsenal, Arsenal". A couple weeks later I will learn that supporters of almost every club in the top leagues, sing the same song, while changing the club name. For example: "Chelsea FC, we're by far the greatest team the world has seen". Even the third league club's supporters sing: "Leyton Orient FC, we're by far the greatest team the world has seen". All of which are sung with full devotion and belief. Aside from these songs, the only voices we hear come from the grandfather sitting behind us, as he insults the Bolton's players. "Watson! That's not a name, it's a cleaning product!" Johnny blushes. He doesn't like the fact that on her first visit to Arsenal's stadium, his guest would hear such insulting language. "Don't pay attention to him,", he says "he's a redneck. But don't worry, there are very few of them here. I'm truly sorry you needed to hear that kind of language". I want to explain to Johnny that I have heard much worse language in Israeli stadiums in the past, but the whistle blows and we all stand up and clap our hands. The moment is exciting, and I forget what I wanted to say.

In the twelfth minute, Bolton score the first goal of the match, and the supporters behind the goal jump out of their seats with happiness. Twenty-two minutes later, Arsenal equalise. The goal is so unexpected, but the crowd's reaction is even more unexpected in my eyes: all the supporters stand up and applaud. And... that is it. Strangely enough, No one jumps on his neighbour with excitement and no mutual hugs between strangers are seen. The grandfather behind us mumbles a curse at the Bolton supporters, his grandson repeats it, and everyone else around ignore them. I do as the locals and applaud the red players standing up. After we sit back down Johnny explains that, "we have the greatest team in the world".

About five minutes before the half-time whistle, the score is still a draw and a slow flow of supporters starts walking in the direction of the snack bars. It surprises me to see supporters leave their seats so they can be first in line for a drink. What if a goal was to be scored at that exact moment? How could they ever forgive themselves? Half time arrives, and along with it comes a variety of attractions; a green Arsenal dinosaur shoots gifts out of a cannon; the announcer reads out online greetings from the club's official web page: "happy birthday to sweet Christine who is celebrating her twelfth birthday today! Happy anniversary to Jack and Jennifer from Pennsylvania"; a few lotteries take place, promising prizes to whoever is holding a ticket with a certain number on it. One of them is led by a recorded video of non-other than Arsene Wenger, the Gunners admired manager. Later on, the camera passes through the stand and broadcasts supporters' faces on the big screens. The announcer follows the pictures with amusing remarks that make the crowd laugh, like when a tired young girl rests her head on a commercial sign, the announcer calls out: "hello, wake up!" Sixty thousand spectators laugh. The song playing in the background is, Let Me Entertain You by Robbie Williams, is very apt. It exemplifies that entertainment is the club's responsibility. As opposed to other places in the world, nothing here is left to the supporters' mood or chance. Let Me Entertain You! the producers at the Emirates Stadium ask. And sixty thousand supporters comply.

Arsenal score their second goal during the first few minutes of the second half, and a lot of supporters who were delayed at the snack bars, miss it. This is also the last goal of the match. The celebrations are as modest as they were for the first goal; cries of happiness and a standing ovation, but no hugs or wild frenzies are seen. Judging by the faces of emerging Arsenal supporters it would have been hard to figure out which club had just won the match, and secured itself a place in next year's Champions League. But after the match Johnny explained his feelings: "today it all came together. Although I have always been an Arsenal supporter, today for the first time I understood why. It was the best experience in the world. We are undoubtedly the best club in the world."

On Saturday night my suitcase arrives at Johnny's apartment. This is also the time to say goodbye and start travelling alone. I move into a hotel and start working.

Chelsea reserves

Before my first visits to the Arsenal and Chelsea football academies, I manage to purchase tickets to the Chelsea versus Portsmouth match, in the Premier Reserve League. The ride from south London to the Chelsea reserve team's stadium takes about an hour. It's an April late afternoon and the temperature is low. On the pitch, both reserve teams are warming up; the hosts are in their blue kits while the Portsmouth players wearing black. Most of the players are young, between the ages seventeen and eighteen. They have contracts with the clubs and are paid a modest salary. Modest, in football terms, that is. Nevertheless, they have great desire to improve; once this season is over, the management will decide who will get a contract with the first team of the club. Others could be sold or loaned to lower league football clubs in England or abroad. In the worst case – young players would have to rethink their future career. The chance of success are small; the chances of failure are frightening. Some of the senior team's players are injured and on the bench. This league is where they will need to prove themselves before returning to play in front of forty-two thousand spectators, at the Stamford Bridge Stadium. The Reserve League is run like any other league; the scores are kept and a champion is declared at the end of the season. The match is also filmed and broadcasted live to the subscribers of the club's television channel.

The stadium is modest and homey. About a thousand supporters – mostly family members who bothered to travel this far and pay a few pounds at the entrance. Amazingly reserve matches of this kind are able to attract up to twelve thousand people, but not today's match. Across the pitch, in a high sealed room are the match broadcaster and the DJ. Before kick-off, the announcer reads out the team's line-ups and the DJ plays cheerful music. The audience sings along. We Are the Champions, Freddy Mercury sings the all-time favourite hymn. We Are the Champions parents, brothers and sisters, join in happily.

Chelsea start well. There is no doubt that it is the better team of the two. The atmosphere is pleasant. It could have been even more pleasant if it wasn't so cold. I don't recognise most of the players on the pitch. After all this is my first visit to a reserve league match, but I manage to pick up some names from the crowd's cheering. One name is mentioned more frequently than the others; a blue kit player named Scott. "Come on Scott, get the ball!" And Scott does. Number eleven puts on a good show during the first half. At the end of it he also determines the half-time score; 1–0 Chelsea.

I have a small notebook I always carry around with me. I open it on rare occasions when there is something I need to write down so I don't forget it, or if there is a sentence I heard that I would like to quote one day, verbatim. Despite the cold and the risk of frostbite, I take out my notebook and write on its first page: 'number eleven, Scott, reserve team, Chelsea'. One day when Scott is famous, I'll remember where I first saw him play.

The second half looks really good for Scott and he scores another goal. At the end of the match Peter, the coach, gathers his players in a circle. A few seconds later they all clap hands and cheer, one for all and all for one. Scott gets most of the compliments. His parents at the stand are glowing with pride. He was short by only one goal from receiving the match ball as a souvenir, as is the English tradition. But there is no reason to worry about him; Scott Sinclair – now I know his full name – will have plenty of opportunities to prove himself in the future.

Chelsea academy

The night before going to the Chelsea academy for the first time, I couldn't close my eyes. I was terrified. Terrified of the people, of the children and the closed office doors. I was concerned I wouldn't make the train on time to Cobham, where the academy is situated. I didn't know who should I ask for upon my arrival, what questions should I ask? At a late night hour I remembered that I forgot picking up my clothes from the dry cleaners. That is how I found myself at an early morning hour, wearing a pair of jeans and a plain T-shirt that were soaked from the local rain – as the dry cleaner wasn't open that early. My body was trembling all the way from the train station to the football academy from the cold. Or maybe it was fear.

The Chelsea academy facilities are located just beside the first team training facilities. Eight words engraved on the entry gates to the building. The words are: Excellence, Pride, Style, Professionalism, Passion, Integrity, Unity and Leadership. Those are the values everyone that sets foot through these gates, should aspire to. At the entrance, I take my time and remove the mud from my shoes. A tall lad, wearing a blue long-sleeve shirt, walks out of the building, greets me, and holds the door open for me. A warm breeze surrounds me; maybe it's the heating system, or just the kind gesture. The first floor is mostly used as the lobby and the entrance to the players' dressing rooms. I walk up to the second floor, looking at the walls that are decorated with professional photos of children of different ages, wearing the club's blue uniform. The heart of the activities is on the second floor, which is covered with blue wall-to-wall carpets. All around us are pictures of the academy's alumni: Scott Sinclair, Ben Sahar and others. Other pictures show local heroes, such as John Terry, the first team's captain, running past Steven Gerrard, the Liverpool FC captain. All through the hallway in front of us are offices with men and woman glued to their computer screens. Most of the doors are closed, so that the children's noise won't bother their work. A big pool table and a plasma TV screening 24-hour sports news are situated in the centre of the floor, alongside a coffee table, offering hot and cold drinks. A big window overlooks a training pitch. An inner modest room with three long dining tables and a small kitchen serves as the academy's dining hall. A second TV screen is hanged on the inner wall.

Local members are easily identified. Some of them wearing shirts with the club's crest and speaking in professional terms are the academy staff. Some are walking in and out the offices and others are seen in the corridors with the academy children, offering advice, a good word and a smile. The young children wearing the same colour kits are the academy's children. At the moment they are chatting amongst themselves, in local slang, and playing pool. The remaining adults are the children's parents. They are grouped by the coffee corner, discussing the children's progress and chatting about day-to-day issues. The only one wearing jeans and a simple T-shirt, with a terrified look in her eyes, not talking to anyone, is me. I don't fit into any of these groups.

Douglas, the general manager, to whom I have already spoken, isn't in today. The door to Steve's office, the acting director of the academy, is open. I gather my courage, walk in and introduce myself. Steve is on his way down to the pitches, but he makes time to talk to me and even bothers to get me the academy's next season schedule. His smile is genuine and his behaviour is surprisingly friendly; "feel free to show up at any time. I'll let the security office know about it", he says. After five minutes of flowing conversation I forget what I was so scared about.

The desk next to Steve's is occupied by Tommy, the academy head scout, and head of the recruiting department. Tommy is kind and welcoming. When Steve leaves the office, I ask him a few questions and he kindly answers all of them. "The scouting department can be divided into three: local scouting, national scouting and international scouting. On the local level Chelsea has about ten people, whose job is to locate children from the age of six, who live in the academy's residency. Usually they would locate them by attending amateur league matches and the friendly matches between state schools. British law states that children that train at the academy must live within a hundred kilometre radius, because they attend state school and arrive at the academy at the afternoon hours. Half a dozen national scouts are trusted with locating children from the ages of fourteen all over Britain. If needed, a foster family will be found for the child until he is independent".

The load of details begins to confuse me. I take my little notebook out. Tommy hands me a pen and waits for a couple second so I can write it all down. Then he continues: "a dozen more scouts operate outside of England. Mostly they attend international youth matches and scout for suitable players there. Today, about thirty percent of the sixteen and over players at the academy are foreigners, and that's about it. If you need anything else, don't hesitate to ask. Don't forget to stop by to say hello the next time you are here, okay?"

At eleven o'clock, when the referees blow their whistles, signalling the kick-off of the matches, I thank Tommy and leave the warm office. The building is quiet now, seeing as all the children are down on the pitches waiting for the matches to start. The parents are on the sidelines, ready to cheer. I step out onto the grounds and take my place alongside one of the pitches. The wind is still blowing and an occasional rain is falling. But suddenly I realise I'm not shivering anymore. Maybe I'm not that cold anymore, maybe I'm not afraid.

Arsenal academy

On Saturday morning the following week, I am on my way to the Arsenal academy for the last week of the current season. This time I remember to get my clothes from the dry cleaners, and I easily find the train I need. I arrive at the academy gate an hour early. On my way I stop at a kiosk and buy the weekend paper, so I have something to pass the time with until the match starts. Forty minutes before kick-off, I walk into the academy. The pitches are still empty and the two-story building is quiet. The academy manager's door is open.

"Mr Smith? Good morning, how are you?" I ask. A chubby man with the facial features of a young man, wearing a blue sweater lifts his head up from a notebook he is reading, and smiles.

"Good morning dear, arrived a little early, haven't you? May I offer you a cup of tea? You could warm yourself up in our guest waiting area or I could show you a little of the academy, if you wish". I wish that very much.

Mr Smith rises from his chair and leads me into the adjacent guest waiting area. "There is a coffee machine at your service and soon enough the staff will start making sandwiches, if you are hungry".

The guest room is warm and cosy. The floor is covered with a red wall-to-wall carpet, and dining tables, with four chairs around each, are arranged perfectly. The outer wall of the waiting room is made of a sliding glass door that leads out to a balcony overlooking the pitches.

"The academy staff sometimes likes to watch the matches from up here. We also host football team managers from many different countries, and they usually love standing up here. When it rains the parents meet here on this balcony, although they prefer being on the sidelines, by their boys".

A small door leads to a study room. In the centre of the room stands a big conference table. Ten sophisticated computers are standing against the surrounding wall. "On weekdays, before practice, the children come here. They bring in their homework from school or practice freely with their workbooks" Mr Smith tells me. "Private teachers are helping and answering questions. The computers are equipped with learning programs so when the children finish with their homework, they are encouraged to engage these programs that are fun as much as educational".

"Are there kids who 'prefer' not to do their homework?" I ask.

"If they have already completed their homework and need no help, they are more than welcome to sit here and play the computers or go outside and play. But that is so only after they are finished with their homework. We make sure our children do not fall back in their school work".

"The academy also has a person responsible for the children's education. Together we decide which subjects to teach and what values to encourage. We usually choose to focus on contents that will develop the young lad's mental abilities; long term thinking, situation analysis. These are features that can help the child on the pitch and throughout their life. If you'd like, you could interview Brian, he is the head of our educational programme".

The easiness and lack of formality of the conversation make me a bit braver: "and what about the children. Could I talk to them?"

"Look, according to the Premier League's rules, the academy children are not allowed to do any kind of interviews, surely you understand. Furthermore, we do not want to expose the children to that kind of experience, at their young age. Throughout the years we will teach them how to deal with the press and with researchers like you. You do understand, don't you? Any other interview you'd might like to do, let me know and I'll have it arranged for you".

It is almost eleven o'clock. The noise of parking cars interrupts our conversation. "Come, I'll give you a tour of the pitches", Mr Smith says, as we go down to the main flight of stairs. The dressing room door opens and closes while boys run in or out, stalling behind for a moment to greet the manager 'good morning'. The two big pitches on the right side of the building are still empty of children. "Most academy heads coach the oldest team in their academy. I coach the 'under 16's." This is the pitch we usually play in. It is standard size, of course. We have a good team this year. I'm optimistic about the odds of sending two or three players to the Arsenal first team in a couple years."

"How many players have you sent so far?" I ask. "We send about two players every year. Usually one of them goes all the way to the Premier League, and the other may be sold to a smaller club in one of the lower leagues. If we manage to sell more players, we are very pleased."

"And selling two players a year is enough to financially justify the operation of such an academy?" I ask.

Mr Smith looks down at me. His smile is more than enough to make me understand that the answer is without a doubt, a positive one.

We continue our tour in the facility. On the west side stands the David Rocastle Dome. The door is open. Inside there is an indoor synthetic grass football pitch. Premier League laws require the academies to have at least one indoor pitch, where children can play when the weather is bad. Training equipment – balls, cones and life size figurines designed to help the children practice their stationary shots – is arranged in the corner of the pitch, outside the lines. Next to the Dome there is another pitch that is different from the rest. On the grass are four goals and it is surrounded by tall fences. "That is our goalies training field," Mr Smith explains. "At almost any hour, you will find at least four goalies training here. The academy employs a total of a two digit number of coaches, a medical staff and fitness coaches, scouts, management people and three gardeners, and if you look to your left, you can see what a good job they are doing".

Ten football pitches are exposed in their full green glory. Mr Smith smiles at me; "beautiful, aren't they?" I ask for permission to take some pictures. Meanwhile, young children start running towards the groomed pitches.

"I must leave," Mr Smith apologizes. "My team is surely ready. Feel free to walk around and take pictures as much as you like. When the matches are over, come inside and have a cup of tea with me".

The pitches are close to one another and I start walking between them, trying to choose which one I am going to stand next to. A small pitch that is separated in two, with young children passing a ball between themselves, catches my attention. A sign announces that this pitch is for the under 10. I cannot take my eyes of them. On the lines, the parents, brothers and sisters are already waiting. I join the line, right next to the corner flag. The children are all wearing the club's kit, the shirt tucked into their shorts, their socks pulled up to their knees. At exactly eleven o'clock, a young referee, with braces on his teeth whistles to mark the beginning of the match. Applause rise from all the pitches simultaneously. The air is full of excitement. The little blue and red players are running around, passing the ball through the centre field and showing impressive skills. The parents cheer constantly, no matter if the move was successful or not.

The Arsenal children are on the attack. A weak ball is kicked towards the goal but the goalkeeper deflects it out. A young player chases it, and when he gets to the ball he hurries back. Suddenly he is standing in front of me. His cheeks are flushed from the effort and at the moment he is focusing all his energy on saying, "could you excuse me..."

I'm embarrassed, not really understanding what David, as the parents on the sideline call him, is asking of me.

"Excuse me..." he says again, not angry and making sure not to come too close. His eyes are focused on the place I'm standing; the corner flag. Within a second I understand and, a little embarrassed about disrupting the match, I move back awkwardly. David sets the ball down on the corner and kicks it wonderfully. I look around the perfect grass; desperately hoping the three perfect gardeners had left a hole for me to crawl into.

When the matches are over I go back up to Mr Smith's office for afternoon tea. The newspaper I bought this morning is still on the table, unopened, exactly as I left it an hour ago. The 'under 16' team did great, Mr Smith tells me.

"And you, did you enjoy your visit?" he asks.

"Very much!" I answer, sparing him the embarrassing incident at the corner flag.

"So, we will we see you next season at the academy, will we?" he asks me the single most stirring question anyone ever asked me before.

Family dinner

The end of the 2006–07 football season will soon enough make way for the summer vacation. Next season, I will already be a regular guest at football matches and a recognised face at the academies. During my three weeks in England I achieved most of my goals; I watched an Arsenal match at the Emirates stadium and a Reserve League match; but, most importantly, I met two academy heads and got their kind permission to undertake my research at their academies next season. Shortly before I will leave England for a short vacation at home, I am invited to dine at Johnnys' family home. I dress up nicely and bring flowers. As appropriate for northern Londoners, all the family members are fans of Arsenal. Johnny's mother is the most enthusiastic of them all. During dinner she makes sure to update her boys with any news regarding the club. We start the meal with some crackers and freshly bought salads from Tesco.

Johnny tells me a bit more about himself; he is an aspiring filmmaker, only a few years older than me, who has his whole future ahead of him. Three years ago he graduated from one of the best film schools in England, and since then he has been looking for a suitable movie script; it needs to be interesting, but not catchy; dramatic but not predictable, romantic but not corny. He is taking his time to find the perfect story to tell. In the meantime – until luck, fortune or an inspiration hit, whichever is the secret to success – Johnny works as a bartender at a little restaurant in order to pay the bills. His education has left him with not much other than financial debts and a free membership to the cinema. He has just gotten back from the cinema and he shares the movie experience with us; this scene was good, that one a little less. "It was nice", he concludes. "But I would have done it much better".

Right across from me sits Roy, Johnny's younger brother and the family's youngest son. He is only in his mid-twenties but his career is almost completely behind him. When he was younger he was scouted as a promising future football player; but that promise disappeared, and with it went the family's spark of happiness. He spends most of his days taking instructional courses in children's football training. His evening hours pass by listening to his father bickering about how close he was to fulfilling the dream.

"You should interview Roy," his father exclaims, through a mouth full of crackers. "He knows a thing or two about the football academies". In a much more silent sarcastic voice, he continues: "too bad it stopped there."

Roy ignores him. He is used to it. "Of course, anything you need," he tells me.

Roy has his father's body type: tall and muscular. His face is delicate, with a touch of his mother's skin tone. He has a diamond earring in his left ear, and I could easily picture him in a big English sports magazine. I don't know how he plays football but he definitely has the football player charm.

While the mother brings out the main course, Spaghetti Bolognese, Roy tells me about his football carrier. He was an attacking midfielder, with an extraordinarily accurate shot. For a couple of years he was the Crystal Palace academy's biggest talent. And then, out of nowhere, during one of the pre-season matches, he twisted his knee while trying to reach a ball that flew behind him.

At this point his mother butted into the conversation. "I was in the crowed, I could hear the dislocation of the knee all the way to where I was sitting. To this day I get the chills whenever I think about it. It was horrible!" and his father adds: "all you needed was an ounce of luck. We could have left this hole and move to the city ages ago. Just an ounce of luck," he concludes with tomato sauce splashing onto his angry face.

After his recovery, Roy had no place at Crystal Palace. He was sent on trial in Iceland, South Africa, and even in Israel. Iceland was too cold for him. How could anyone play in that weather anyway? South Africa was hotter and he almost made it there, but then he fell in love with a British girl from his neighbourhood and decided to stay home and be with her. After they broke up, as first lovers often do, he was sent on trial in Israel.

He was sure he was going to make it there and even make "Aliyah". He stayed with one of his mom's sisters; she has plenty of family in Israel. But somehow... the alarm clock didn't ring and he was late to the final and most important practice.

"What can you do..." the feminine voice interjects again. "I raised two spoiled children that don't like working hard". She knows something about working hard as she spent her entire childhood in a Kibbutz.

"Love stories always end up ruining everything," Johnny adds. He probably lacks a bit romance in order to become a truly successful film producer.

"That has nothing to do with it!" the father concludes the conversation. With a mouth full of strawberry pie and chocolate ice cream he says: "All that was missing was an ounce of luck. An ounce of luck and we could all have quit our jobs, sit at home and watch football all day."

David

At that dinner I met David. David is a Jewish football player who came all the way from Spain to England in order to play at a local academy. When Roy's career as a professional footballer ended, he decided to become a youth coach, on one of the training sessions Roy and his classmates visited Arsenal's academy. It was there that he met David, and their paths haven't parted since. David lives with a foster family in the northern part of London and he is really happy there. But the foster family doesn't share his religion and, once in a while, when David misses home, he is invited to Jonny's parents' house, for some food and companionship. There he feels like the youngest brother.

David has fair hair and skin. When he arrived at the academy he was skinny, but today after rigorous training in the gym, supervised by the coach, doctor and dietician, he has built himself a fit and muscular body. He is a little over seventeen and a half years old, which is a little older then when Roy finished his carrier. The academy heads foresee a bright future for David. He will probably be part of the first generation to graduate under the academy's new structure. In the meantime they are asking for his patience. And despite dreaming about the day he will step onto the pitch at the Emirates Stadium for the first time, David has much patience. For now, he follows instructions; he trains the way the academy tells him to train and eats what they tell him to eat. David is a good lad, exactly as lads at the academy are expected to be.

He insists on being modest despite the fact that he has all the reasons to be big-headed about himself in a country that worships football players. He rarely goes out to party at night and when he does, he never comes back after midnight. In his spare time he catches up on studying Spanish history, which he missed when he moved to England. He has a new car, not too flashy, and he makes sure to drive safely. When we met, at the end of the football season, he was starting to think about next year. Will he go up to the first team squad or will he stay another year at the academy? In any case he will continue coming to Friday dinners at Roy's house. If he would have graduated the academy a few years back, there was no question about his future, according to the opinion of some experts. He would have at got into the first team squad immediately at the age of eighteen; he would probably train with them on a regular basis though spending most of the matches on the bench, fighting for a spot in the starting eleven. However, during the last couple of years the academy has made some changes and now they nurture the young children and keep them under a protective wing until the age of twenty-one. The logic behind this decision is simple; it is much preferred that the young potential plays a couple more years in the reserve league, or be loaned to a team in a lower division, where he will improve his skills while playing competitive matches. So as for today, David does not know what the future holds for him. It might be a while before he gets the opportunity to walk down the tunnel at the Emirate Stadium.

David has already trained with the first team a couple of times. At the end of the training, Arsene Wenger, the manager, worked with him on his skills and suggested working on free-kicks. Wenger asked, and David spent long hours kicking dozens of balls into the night. Roy did all he could to help. Sometimes he collected balls and sometimes he stood between the goalposts and gave advice. Now that his career is over, David's success is his success. David's next year at the academy will determine his future, as will it determine Roy's.

Dinner is followed by a round of affectionate goodbyes. This is David's last weekend at Roy's family home. This is also my last night in the city.

Around ten pm Johnny and Roy's father offer to drive David and me to the tube. The two friends say goodbye with a last warm hug. I say my goodbyes to Johnny, Roy and the rest of the family. We all promise to meet again in a few months.

The next morning, during my flight back to Israel, I think about David's future and about what he is yet to face. I think about Roy also, how he missed his big break as a professional football player and about Johnny's heartfelt love of a football club, which he will never make a movie about, as 'football movies have long became so corny', I can almost hear him answer. I remember Steve and Tommy from the Chelsea academy, and Mr Smith from the Arsenal academy. With weary fingers I open my notebook and read the only name I have written in it: Scott, number 11, Chelsea reserve team. At some point between Italy and Tel-Aviv I leave all the foreign names behind and all I can think of is home. The stress, burden and excitement of returning finally overtake me and I slip into a blurry haze of sweet dreams.

August – September 2007
Tuition Fee

Tom

Three months after my first visit to the city, I return to London. It is the middle of the summer holidays and the atmosphere in the football academies is pleasant. The first team players are probably still working on their tan at some exotic resort around the world, but the young academy boys are already working hard, waiting for the start of the season impatiently. The academy heads use the summer to trial new players for the upcoming season. This is exactly the reason why 16-year-old Tom Gannot came here all the way from Israel. Arik Yahalomi, which is the unofficial representative of the Israel Football Association in England, is also an agent of young players, agreed, and I found myself joining in the journey of a young ambitious boy towards his dream.

The journey's dramatic peak arrived on a sunny afternoon, at the end of August. Arik asked Tom to get into the car and listen very carefully, and so Tom did. He knew this was the moment he had been waiting for years.

"I talked to the head" Arik started in his typical dramatic tone. Of course we knew that; up until a moment ago Tom and I were watching the two gentlemen whispering in somewhat mysterious tones. They were standing a short distance from us and we couldn't hear what they were saying, although we knew. During that short talk on the green lawn, under London's sun, they arranged the future of the young boy who is sitting next to me now. While Arik was telling us what was said, we didn't dare disturbing him in any way.

"I have news for you, young man" he said, "some is good and some is bad".

I can't imagine what was going through Tom's mind during these moments, waiting to hear whether the Watford academy head thought he was good enough to play in his prestigious academy next season.

Tom Gannot is a player in the youth department of Hapoel Petach-Tikva, a first division football club in Israel. He is only sixteen and yet has already played in a couple of games with the Israeli club's first team. He plays as a right defensive midfielder and can also play in a more attacking role. He has been in London for three weeks already. He came on trial to two of the Championship academy clubs: Queens Park Rangers and Watford. QPR said 'Thank you, but not this year.' after seeing him play in two matches. Watford is his last chance in England. If he doesn't get in he will go back to Israel. In the meanwhile, he is here, at the beautiful Watford training facility, waiting to hear the news his agent has for him. Some bad and some good.

During the last week, summer had arrived in London and the bright sun is hitting our faces. Tom just got out of his ice bath, a masochistic habit of football players meant to prevent muscle cramps after physical exertion. He is still sweating though, maybe it's the sun and maybe it's Arik's dramatic voice. That morning Tom played with the Watford academy against Oxford's academy. He has only played few minutes during the second half, and he wasn't bad at all. Tom is at least a year younger than the rest of the players in the team, and his body is not as fit as theirs. And if that's not enough, the players constantly speak in a fast fluent English, swallowing syllables. Later he will tell us that communicating was hard for him.

"But you know... that's football. You keep playing". And when Tom played, he even called out to his teammates in English. He settled himself in midfield and moved a little up field. On two occasions he even shoots the ball towards the net. He did a good job in defence as well. His disadvantage, however, is one-on-one. The Oxford players realised that early in the match and pressured him heavily whenever he had the ball. It didn't look so good. During the last period, he still had a hard time adjusting.

"The coach changed the formation", he will tell us later, "and I didn't really understand what he said."

It's not easy to be tested in a foreign country; eight out of the eleven team players have been playing together for years. As a new player he needed to integrate himself into their existing formation, and even to rise above them while doing so. Moreover, there is the language and communication barrier, the physical differences and the different game style. Tom has to face it all, and it is unclear whether he succeeds.

We are sitting in the air-conditioned car waiting for his agent's declarations.

"The bad news is that according to this match the answer is no. You have football in you, no one can question that, and your skills don't fall short of anyone else's here. But that is not enough; you need to be a lot better than them. The good news, however, is that you are given another chance. You are invited to play again on Saturday, against the Brighton academy. If you show a little more determination and strength, with better one-on-one skills we will have something to talk about". Arik concluded his news as both Tom and my breath was taken for the next two days.

Saturday, the Watford academy hosts the Brighton academy. Tom is not starting the game. The Brighton academy dominated the match and by the end of the first thirty minutes, lead 3-0. Tom doesn't get his chance during the first hour. I spend the half-time break playing football with little Mat, trying to release the pressure of two days and sixty minutes without breath. Mat is nine years old and quite lean, but with potential to grow during the next couple of years. During the weekdays Mat attends the local academy, but on weekends, he prefers watching his friends practice in the academy instead of going to the first teams' matches. Mat requests that I will shoot the ball at him while he stands between the goalposts. My skills are nothing to be proud of and Mat easily manages to block all of the shots. In between shots we talk football.

"The Watford team doesn't really interest me, but I'm really attached to its academy. To tell you the truth, I don't think I am good enough, and I have a feeling I will not keep playing here next season. I'll be sad, of course I'll be sad. But I won't stop coming here to watch my friends play".

Tom goes on to play at the beginning of the last third of the game, taking his place in midfield. The team looks better. Tom shoots towards the net once and assists two players to score. Compared to the last game, his improvement is easily seen. He seems to understand that this is his last chance. But while he displays great individual skills he neglects his teamwork and tactical discipline. At every chance he gets, no matter how far he is from the goal, he tries to score. By doing so, Tom makes his team lose some valuable opportunities. The game ends with the score of 3–1 to Brighton.

The answer hasn't changed after the match. The Watford academy, as did QPR, both rejected Tom by saying, "thank you, but it's still no. Go back to Israel and play in the first team. One day, if you keep getting stronger, maybe you can come back and play with us."

A couple of hours later we drop Tom at the airport. The evening darkness has already swallowed all spark of light and despair is overtaking hope. I hate airports; the noise, confusion and millions of people.

"You know, I'm not sad," Tom whispers to his agent and me, a second before he walks into departures. "I came here, I tried, and I know that one day I will succeed. Do you hear that? I will be back one day," he whispers, in the middle of this loud and busy airport, with thousands of people walking past us every minute, we heard him.

Alan Sefton

August is Alan Sefton's busiest month of the year. Alan is the head of the 'Arsenal in the community' department. The department has been active for the last twenty-two years with him as its head. During the first few years it dealt with the neighbourhood's local community. As the years went by the department grew and today it operates all over London, England and many other countries worldwide. The department works all year round and during August it hosts an international football tournament, which is the club's pride.

Sefton tells me: "Today, every major company in the world operates in the community. Through the department Arsenal tries to compensate for the environmental damages it causes; pollution and noise. We also feel that we need to give back to the community we live in. Arsenal residents suffer inconveniences, especially on match days; they suffer troubles with parking, plus all the garbage and noise the sixty thousand fans create surely damages their weekend routine. These past few years we've decided to expand our activity with the hope of reaching as many places as we can internationally. That's because Arsenal has supporters all over and it is in the club's interest to keep its good reputation.

"Today, Arsenal Football Club is an international company. Even though the team plays only in England, its management is spread all around the globe, as are the marketing, advertising and community departments.

Our department is not measured by its financial profits, but by the amount and quality of social and communal activities we take part in.

"Arsenal's community projects are varied. Once every couple of weeks, a few of the first team players are asked to contribute a number of hours to the community. They are sent to visit the homes of disabled children or help the elders renovate their houses. Each of these visits brings great excitement for those who are assisted and for the players themselves. To be honest, some players are much more motivated to volunteer then others. They are the first to offer themselves in any activity we do. It is a little harder with less motivated players, so we try to offer them activities they can enjoy as well. We try and make sure that everyone is happy at the end of the day.

"In addition to the club's volunteer work, the Premier League collaborates with a dozen of other community associations. Players from all football clubs in the Premier League take their turn and help renovate low budget schools or visit hospitals and homes for the elderly. Volunteering has become an integral part of English football.

"Ten years ago we started a programme for helping local children with their studies after school. We started with private teachers that spent time with the children working on their homework. As time went by our teachers started using football scenarios in order to make the material more interesting for the children. Today we are in close contact with the British Department for Education, who purchased the programmes of teaching we created. Our methods are proving themselves; when we want to teach the children about reading and writing, we let them work with Arsenal stories. They much rather read about that then about England during the Roman era. Our programmes are relevant to almost every field; when we want to teach children maths we use the numbers of the players so, Instead of asking how much is four plus fifteen, we ask how much is Fabregas plus Danielson. We teach geography using our rival teams or the countries where players have come from. Recently, we filmed Fabregas talking about the city of Barcelona, his hometown. That way we make the subject attractive to the children and it gives us an advantage over any other conventional teaching programme.

"During these last couple of years we started a language programme. The

British children do not have to learn a second language in school. We are trying to encourage them to do so. Fortunately, Arsene Wenger is a linguist and has a vast interest in languages. He has been very helpful in raising the awareness to this matter. Subjects such as health, nutrition and even cooking, have become very popular in the education system, and we take example from the players' diet to help teach these subjects.

"Football today is a highly popular sport. Using the game we can reach all the children in the educational system. Some children weren't infected with the sports bug at home, but by learning reading, writing, maths and languages through our programmes, we hope that they will become fans of the game and later on, of course, we hope they grow up to be Arsenal supporters.

"It could be claimed that the club makes financial profits from these activities, growing our future fan base in England. But that is not the reason we do it. At the end of the season we are not measured in financial term, like other departments. In many of our programmes we expect no profit whatsoever. When we open a project in Kenya, for example, we know that the chance of seeing a financial profit out of it is next to nil. Kenyan children cannot afford to buy an original Arsenal jersey for forty pounds a piece. The most they can afford is buying a fake T-shirt for one pound, in which case we make no profits at all".

Arsenal operates football schools in many countries in the world including England of course. Schools that are located outside of England are managed by the local clubs, whereas Arsenal's contribution is in training the team's coaches and constructing special training programmes for the young players, that originate from Arsenal Football Club. Arsenal provides its name and training programmes, and the local school commits to follow its guidelines. In most of these schools, the programmes are not free, and the children pay to take part in them, so Arsenal gets a percentage of the revenue. However, in some schools Arsenal asks for no profit. These are disadvantaged places, like the children's hospital in Chernobyl, Ukraine and a couple of cities in South Africa, Kenya and Israel.

Recently a few of these projects were initiated in Israel, sponsored by the club. One of them is a Jewish/Muslims project, aiming to generate a dialog between the communities. When we start talking about the project, Sefton's practical manner turns into a worried Jewish grandfather: "I have family in the Galilee, and every time I go visit them my heart shrinks. The Galilee is filled with Jewish and Muslims settlements, that are situated one next to the other, but their children keep going to separate schools… The goal of this project is to bring neighbours closer so we created twin settlements where children from all religions could play football together. Once a year we bring them here for a week long tour in London and an international tournament. I personally hope that this project will make a difference", Alan Sefton concludes.

Arsenal's football tournament

Each year, a hundred and twenty football teams from across the globe attend the Arsenal football tournament, which aims to encourage friendships and international collaborations. The Israeli team in this year's tournament is made up of mixed Jewish and Muslim Israeli children. The peak of their week came on the fourth day of the tournament. So far our two teams, The Galilee Gunners and The Galilee Vampires, have lost every game they played, meaning they are placed last in the league table. That day the Galilee Gunners were leading 3–2 until the eighty-fifth minute of the game. Those three goals against the Danish team were more than both teams had scored during the entire tournament. Each goal made the parents in the crowd and the players on the bench jump with joy. Even the Vampires, who were playing on the adjacent pitch and were already losing 2–0, stopped once in a while to cheer their fellow teammates. Then, in the eighty-fifth minute, the Gunners conceded a silly goal that tied the game. After the whistle was blown, the players headed towards penalty kicks, to determine the winner. The toss of a coin determined that the team from Denmark would go first. When the first Danish kicker approached the ball, all the Vampires and Gunners stood next to each other, hugging in one line, with a determined look in their eyes.

They didn't all know each other at first. Despite spending a three-day training camp together, it was still pretty challenging to bridge the language gap between two nationalities, more so when having to deal with a third language in a foreign country. It was hard, but also quite funny. During the opening games, when the referee whistled a player, trying to explain, in

English of course, what his offence was, the Israeli player stood there with his head bowed and a shamed look on his face. Not because of the bad offense but because he didn't understand a word the referee was saying.

"Tell him 'sorry', tell him 'sorry'," he heard yelled from the bench, so he said 'sorry'. On a different occasion, one of the players was positive he wasn't the last one to touch the ball before it left the pitch so he called: "our ball, our ball", in Hebrew. He looked surprised when the referee gave him a bewildered look.

During the couple of days prior to that game, mainly during lunch breaks, the two Israeli teams practiced cheering rituals that happen after a goal. They picked a player that was most likely to score and ran after him trying to hug him. It's good that they tried it off the pitch because they didn't have a chance to get so cheerful during the formal games, not even once… They did, however all hold their heads in frustration numerous times after conceding three, four and even seven goals in one game.

Then came the game against Denmark, where they were only five minutes away from a first sensational victory. The Danish were the first to shoot, and they scored. Jeremy, one of the Israeli teams' prominent players, walks over to the white dot, takes his penalty, and scores, 1–1. It is the Danes turn to shoot. The Israeli goalkeeper, Abed, who's quiet compact in size, possesses some impressive goalkeeping skills. High shots, though, give him a hard time. This one wasn't so high, but Abed, for some reason, concedes. It's 2–1 to Denmark. The players in white didn't manage to score with their next two shots. The Danes however, actually did score, and so, this is how close the Israeli football team came to winning its first game.

Modern history tells us that football has been a means of recruiting the masses to take part in revolutions and social protest in the past and nowadays, it's still used to boost the national spirit and patriotism of the citizens. In the last couple of years, football has also recruited for community purposes. Seemingly, twenty-two players that do not play football very well, have nothing to do in an international tournament arranged by Arsenal Football Club. But only seemingly; because sometimes it is not the only thing that matters. Nobody in London remembers little Guy's shot with the toe of his boot instead of the inner foot for the worst. Twenty-two children along with their professional staff and escorting parents have other memories that have little to do with football. They savour the tours of London and laugh together in the big green parks. The karaoke night is also an evening they'll remember, all the jokes they managed to tell each other half in Hebrew and half in Arabic... At night, they couldn't sleep because of being too excited from the huge magnificent pitches, the kits and the rival teams that couldn't stop crossing their minds. When they finally fell asleep, they separately dreamt mutual dreams about becoming professional football players when they grow older. And football, that could also use to recruit people for war, is reflected so brightly in these little boys' eyes, while standing there, hugged in one line, dreaming about scoring the last penalty goal, so that they can cheer and celebrate like they rehearsed before. Maybe one day they will learn how to shoot with the inner part of the foot. Until then they have learned other things that matter none the less, as mutual respect, friendship and cooperation with no regard to race or religion.

Maccabi Tel-Aviv

During August, Maccabi Tel-Aviv's youth team arrives for a visit in London. They were invited to play against a couple of academies in the city. On their first day in London, they play against the Chelsea academy. They are tired, but excited. Maccabi Tel-Aviv's players take to the pitch wearing the team's yellow kit, for a match against Chelsea's blue team. It is a cold, rainy day, and the Israeli players who dreamt about playing under 'European conditions', are quite happy with it. The substitutes are sitting in silence on the Chelsea bench. The team's coach is standing confidently on the lines, watching every move. Maccabi Tel-Aviv's young players are half sitting half standing beside the bench next to two of the escorting parents who function as coaches. There's the video cameraman and there's me. All other parents are standing on the other side of the pitch.

The referee talks to both captains in English. The Israeli team captain nods his head and the Israeli players shake hands with all three officials. Later on the Israeli players are asked to stand in a row while the local team walks by, shaking their hands. Chelsea's children are thirteen years old but look about one size bigger than Maccabi Tel-Aviv players.

The first goal of the match, which happens early on in favour of

Maccabi Tel-Aviv is a result of the London goalkeeper abandoning his goal posts too soon. Cheers of joy came from the bench and improvised supporters' stands. At first, the parents try to calm the players, reminding them, "this is just a friendly game". At some point they give up; "how often do they get to score against the great Chelsea? Let them celebrate!" Chelsea score twice and takes the advantage. During the last few minutes of the game the Israeli team scores a goal from within the box. It is not clear whether the ball crossed the line or not, but the referee declares it legal and the score is a tie. The players and parents are ecstatic. The referee whistles for the end of the match and hosting team do not leave the pitch, as they are waiting for the traditional handshakes. In the meantime, the Israeli team are far away and deep in celebration. The Chelsea team gives up; shake the referees' hand and heads towards the dressing room.

Two days later Maccabi Tel-Aviv are matched against the Leyton Orient academy from League One. They beat the hosting academy 5–1. When the match is over the children hurry over to the heated bus, ignoring the English manners once again. The next day, the Israeli team heads north to the Watford training facility. The Watford academy children are as good as the Chelsea players. Maccabi players are the first to score, taking advantage of a sloppy defence by the Watford goalkeeper, causing the locals to hold their heads in anguish. Throughout the match Watford ties the score but during the last few minutes, a long distance shot beats the local goalkeeper and Maccabi win 2–1. The referees whistle, heard a split second after the ball hits the net, sets the beginning of the celebrations. The Watford kids don't give up. They wait for the celebrations to fade and insist on shaking the hands with the Israeli team. "Good game, good game," the team in the black kits compliment the visiting one.

The next match, against the West Ham academy, is a match the Israeli team would like to forget. At the beginning of the match they are still cheerful from the last few matches. They score first and celebrate as usual. Soon enough the West Ham team come to its senses and by playing a patient and organised game wins the first half with a 7–1 score. The final score of the game is 11–1. Despite the disappointed feeling, the Maccabi children stand together for a friendly group photo and handshakes.

On the last day of the visit, the youth team is invited to play against

Maccabi London amateur team. It's Sunday and the sidelines are packed with Jewish and Israeli parents, blabbing about this and that in English spiced with some phrasing from the holy land. It is an exciting event for everyone. During the first half, the Israeli team scores enough goals to ensure a victory. The coaches reorganise the players a bit to balance strength between the two teams. Uri, a young curly blonde boy, joins the local team. While he is on the pitch, he arranges the defence and attack of the English children. He even threatens his friend's goal a couple of times. When he scores, he celebrates modestly. At the end of the day all of the players go to a traditional kosher lunch. I accompany Uri along the way from the pitch to the dressing rooms. We chat in Hebrew for a while when a British blond haired boy with flushed cheeks shows up. He extends his hand to Uri and says: "I wanted to thank you for playing with us." Uri is confused at first because of the foreign language but after a quick translation he shakes the young boy's hand and answers: "you're welcome!"

Two months later, during a visit is Israel, I arrive at Maccabi Tel-Aviv's training facility, to watch the team play in their home ground. The facility is so poor compared to those they have in England. The parking lot is packed with cars parked crookedly while the drivers are honking impatiently. The distance to the pitch is far and the pitches are separated by tall fences. The players, however, don't devote their attention to environmental distractions. Their heads are held high on the pitch, their chests are puffed out and their feet are light. They beat the visiting team with no difficulty, modestly celebrating each goal they score. When the referee whistles for the end of the match, they walk over to their guest team players, shake their hands, and thank them for the effort they made and for the match. I believe the short visit in England can take credit for this nice gesture.

Being a football supporter before the twenty-first century

QPR

With all due respect to this gentlemanlike, civilised and good-cause orientated English football, where is the famous, violent hooliganism in English football that books and movies were written about? I want to hear about uncompromising local identity, about manly brotherhood decorated with sweat, brawling and broken teeth. Where do I start looking? Obviously not in the football academies, nor at the community-focussed international tournaments. After my first football match with Johnny, I figured out that I wouldn't find it at the Emirate Stadium either. So I decided to look elsewhere. Queens Park Rangers is a club from the lower half of the second league (the Championship). They started this season with many hopes and many fears.

On a cool evening, in mid-September, I make my way to central London. I don't know the way to the Loftus Road Stadium but am hoping the crowd coming out of the Tube with me will lead me there. Unfortunately, when I step out of the station, there are barely ten people around me wearing random coloured T-shirts. Not quite what I expected. They are all walking in the same direction, but is it the one I need? I ask for help from a young supporter with a kind face, wearing a red coat. "Yes, that's the way. Is this your first time at the stadium? Welcome." We leave the station and walk past a couple of building and privet vegetable gardens. The road is not so short, I think to myself. Is he sure this is the right way? And how would I have found it on my own?

"Most of the supporters are usually local." He tells me. "Only few foreigners show up here. This is a community club, everyone knows everyone," he explains. "So, tell me, where are you from? You came all the way from Israel to watch a QPR match? That's Great! Don't worry, next time you'll find your way just fine."

At some point we come across a blocked road. Only Pedestrians walk here. More people join us, and the strong floodlights coming from the stadium decorate the quiet street with a festive look. Teddy, my pleasant tour guide, shows me where the ticket booth is located and bids me goodbye. "I'll see you at the next match. Do come, OK?"

The clock shows that I have fifteen minutes left until the kick-off whistle. The line moves quickly. I pay twenty pounds and get a slip of paper in return, with the ticket details printed on it in tiny letters. I start walking towards one of the gates with the ticket in my hand.

I show my ticket to the security guard at the entrance to block eight. The guard, a tall, with the initial impression of a scary guy, looks at the paper I handed him. He signals 'no' with his head after a few long seconds. Few more second later he says: "come with me." A little frightened, I do as he says. During the short walk, while holding my ticket, he starts questioning me.

-      "Which team are you here to see?"
-      "The local one," I answer quickly.
-      "Are You a Queens Park Rangers supporter?"
       He doesn't sound convinced. I nod.
-      "Who did you come with?" he inquires.
-      "Alone". As simple as that.
-      "Why?"

I don't understand the purpose of his questioning and what confession is trying to get out of me, but I start getting nervous. Have I done something wrong? Does the security guard suspect I want to join a hooligan gang? I ask myself. While I try figuring out the answers in my head, the guard stops and stands in front of me. His big body blocks a light coming from behind him and making a big shadow on the wall, making him look even more frightening. He stares at me for a few long seconds. I remember he is still waiting for an answer. "Umm...I don't know what you mean..." I confess.

"I was asking, how is it, that a nice girl like yourself hasn't found someone to go with to a football match", he smiles widely and hands me my ticket. "Here you go, this is block six. This is where your seat is. Enjoy the match", he says, then turns and disappears in the direction we just came from. What a relief.

After my heart settles back to its normal rhythm, I walk into the stadium through gate six and find my seat; number ninety-seven, sixth row. I'm so close to the pitch that I can hear the player's voices and see their body stretch while preparing for a kick. A human sized mascot, something between a black cat and a monkey, is standing by the sidelines and jokes around with the crowd, shaking hands with some of them, taking pictures with others. Then I pick an old couple walking into the stadium, the women is holding a mascot, somewhere between a cat and a monkey. The big mascot asks them for her miniature replicate and hangs it on the corner post of the gate. Later on he picks a little boy out of the crowd and brings him over to the mascot hung on the corner post. He tells him to grab the mascot, but once the boy reaches for it, he teases him and moves the mascot a bit higher so it will be out of reach, then he swings him away. When the child finally reaches the doll, the big mascot asks him to throw it back to the nice granddaddy who bought it in the first place. This entertaining flirt goes on to the crowd's enjoyment until kick-off.

During the match, the QPR football players bring much less satisfaction to their crowd then the pre-match entertainment did. They make no real attempt to score. They rarely have control on the ball. In fact, Plymouth, the opposing team, probably didn't score this time thanks to the strong wind blowing in their faces and not because of QPR good defensive abilities. The stadium is only half full and most of the supporters are seated in the higher seats or behind the goals. The team's performance, together with the referee's blowing the whistle every few seconds, manage to excite the crowd; the shouting becomes louder as the frustrations grows but the overall atmosphere is good. Around thirty minutes into the match, when the team is looking even worse than it did at the beginning, the supporters burst into song: "We're by far the greatest team the world has ever seen"… And they sing the chorus with such faith, that even while looking at their team playing this dull match, one would have a hard time not believing every word they sing.

I look at the supporters next to me and at in the stands behind me, and try to find some of the hooligans that I have heard so much about but never came across. No sign of any of them. At this point, everyone is singing a love song to QPR, even the old couple! The woman is enthusiastically moves the mascot's mouth move along with the words of the song: "We're by far the greatest team the world has ever seen".

During half-time, a second entertainer walks to the pitch, holding a microphone. "It is time to entertain you," he calls to the crowd. Four young men are picked from the crowd. The announcer declares a competition. Each one of them will spin a long stick for thirty seconds and then try to score a penalty kick. The winner will win a new television. Each participant gets two attempts but only one, wearing the official team's jersey, scores twice. Watching this from the stands is painfully hilarious. When the competition is over and the winner is declared, we all go on cheering him for a couple of long minutes after. The second half kicks-off with a much happier mood than when the first one ended.

Queen Park Rangers keep up with their poor performance, and now, with the wind in their faces, they fail to protect the net. Twice. The supporters are quite angry now. Some of them shout out towards the players and the referee. Following one of the referee's calls, one of the supporters standing above me, gets pretty upset and throws down his match programme, which he has just bought at the entrance. This violent act catches the supporters next to me, by surprise. After looking up in bewilderment, one of the supporters picks up the programme, brushes it off and puts it in his pocket as if it was worth a fortune.

Forty-five minutes later, the local supporters start leaving the stadium, disappointed. "See you next season I guess," a supporter next to me tells his friend playfully, "let's hope it won't be in the Third Division."

The journey back to north London takes about an hour. During the ride I try to understand what happened to the violent British football experience that was so rooted in this culture. Has it, as I witnessed at the matches, disappeared in favour of a relatively calm and playful show? Has it been replaced by people dressed up as green dinosaurs and monkey-like cats?

When I get back to my rented room, I lie down on the bed, next to a pile of books talking about the period when football was a working class sport. A movie I bought this morning peeks out of the DVD player. I press the play bottom and fall asleep with Green Street hooligans. I wonder if reading books and watching movies, are the only way I have left to

---

1. Imlach, G., (2005). My Father and Other Working Class Heroes. London: Yellow Jersey Press.

understand the meaning of being an English football supporter up until the 1990s.

My Father and Other Working Class Heroes

Plenty of books and movies have been written about that period in football history. One of them is called My Father and Other Working Class Heroes , which was written by a journalist named Gary Imlach, son of former player Stuart Imlach. Imlach tells about his childhood extensively; the local residents of his childhood neighbourhood would traditionally visit the homes of local team players before the matches, to wish them luck and ask for tickets. The relationship between football players and their supporters was as neighbours. They use to meet in pubs before and after the matches, exchange experiences in the grocery store. Social and economic differences between players and supporters did not exist; at that time, football players, as did their supporters, worked a full day, some as construction workers, and 'job' by the football club he belonged to. This is how it became likely that they could see a great football player play in front of a hundred thousand supporters during the season, and sell lunch in one of the local diners in the summer. You're welcome to imagine Frank Lampard or Rio Ferdinand wear a paper hat and serving you a pecan pie to go in a brown paper bag, pretty unimaginable. But they didn't have a choice then. Until the mid-60s, the maximum wage of a football player who's recognised by the law, was fifteen pound sterling for a week throughout the season. On vacations, it would drop drastically. In 1963 the law was changed, and the wage was raised by five to ten pounds per week, when the record was set on a hundred pounds, paid to Johnny Haynes by Fulham, he was also the captain of the England team back then. Since the sixties, football players' salary increased gradually. It didn't reach the vast numbers we are used to hear nowadays until the nineties. Many years will pass until photos of famous players like Rio Ferdinand wearing a paper hat will become totally unreasonable.

Until the seventies, football players and supporters belonged to the blue-collar working class. There is a scene from the movie Those Glory Glory Days (1983), which is about a north London girl, who supports Tottenham during the sixties, which I vaguely recall; This girl's mom, the wife of a senior official in the city council, who's frustrated by her young daughters hobby, is asking: "Am I the wife of a coal miner?" The mom thinks it's not becoming that the daughter of an honourable family will choose football as her hobby. At that time, football stadiums were not a suitable place for girls, whether because of their gender or because, their young age or because of their social status. The crowd use to stand on the terraces, and a vast amount of supporters would squeeze onto them. A tremendous amount of trash would accumulate under the wooden staircase with only one discarded cigarette butt being enough to create a massive fire trap. The supporters would become a surging human mass each time a goal was scored. They were only restricted by the high fences separating the mass from the pitch. As I said, not an ideal environment for young girls to hang around in.

Football wasn't always a working class game. Until the end of the nineteenth century it was played in aristocrats' Public Schools in England. Although they are called 'public', they are very exclusive and expensive. The tuition in those schools was high and the curriculum was built in order to manufacture men that will one day govern the great British Empire.

The games rules were rather vague and the children pretty much played by their own school's set of rules. In some of them, the player could hold the ball in his hand and physically attack a rival. The final score didn't matter. They encouraged children to play football because it was a great way of teaching them important social values as fair play, teamwork and gentlemen like behaviour. Only in 1863, The Football Association was founded to administer the game, at the same time English society started to have a shorter working week and have a day off for their leisure activities.

In 1885, when football in England first turned into a professional sport, whose participants got paid to play, mainly working class men played it. The upper class embraced some rather more elitist games – rugby, cricket, tennis and polo. These games require expensive equipment that the working class men couldn't afford. A cricket match also takes a few days, which these working class men couldn't waste on playing. With no choice and with the help of an old, heavy leather ball, football became a sport of those who couldn't afford the time and money spent needed for other games. The level of violence at this time was high as well, with the supporters, who hadn't had a proper education, swearing at the officials and the players, expressing their frustration at the poor performance on the pitch with threatening hand movements. This kind of aggressive behaviour was pretty common and even acceptable at football matches at that time, but starting during the 1970s, eighty years after the change in footballs' social status, football hooliganism had begun raising its ugly head. It became more violent, more organised, much more daring.

The Popplewell Report that was published in England in 1984, divided violence in football stadiums into two types: the first type of violence was mostly reactive violence prompted by what happened on the pitch. This type of violence was common throughout the past one hundred years, and it was carried out, it is claimed, from people who were not taught proper social manners. The second type of violence made it first appearance, as mentioned, only in the seventies. This was not a spontaneous kind of violence, related directly to the events on the pitch, rather a planned type of violence, performed by known street gangs, whose actions are unrelated to anything to do with what's going on the pitch.

The match is only an excuse, violence is the main goal. The Popplewell Report states three main characteristics of the organised hooliganism phenomenon: it only existed in England, it only appears in football and it's new. As to the year of writing this report, this is a reliable report, but in the upcoming years, hooliganism will spread in many cities around the world and in other different sports.

A lot of football clubs at that time had a community of supporter, composed of a group of youngsters with a strong sense of local identity, who give uncompromising love towards their favourite football club. Expressions of this uncompromising love were among others, face to face battles against supporter/firms of rival teams. Both teams' supporters used to spend the hours leading up to the match, drinking themselves to the point where their fears and anxieties of physical pain fade away, allowing them to schedule a time and place for the next battle. Deadly weapon however, were never involved; these spontaneous lower class street fighting reflected the English gentlemen-like manners after all. Nevertheless, it was not child's play. They led to injuries, broken bones, loss of consciousness and even death. The supporters equipped themselves with clubs, broken glass bottles and any other weapon they could put their hand on. In some cases they would appear in one of the local pubs, where the rival

---

2. Armstrong, G., (1998). Football Hooligans: Knowing the Score. New York: Oxford. Pgs 108–109

supporters were sitting, and throw improvised smoke bombs inside, meant to 'invite' them to a battle outside. They slowly became more sophisticated with their battle tactics and fighting methods, and would often continue the battles on the field. Offensive chants, which were also racist, were aimed at the rival teams' players and supporters. Dangerous objects were thrown at the referee and the active players on the pitch. When the police started confiscating these objects at the entrance to the stadium, the hooligans found an original way to wound those who they thought deserved it, and started throwing small coins, often with cruelly sharpened edges. Outside the stadium, the supporter gangs caused big environmental damage, they would disrupt buses and trains, cause riots inside the pubs they were sitting in, they would break into stores and steal whatever's their wanted.

The police, who were overwhelmed and helpless, allocating increasing resources to fight this violent. During the football season of 1989/90, nearly ten million pounds was invested in police enforcement with around five thousand officers spread in and outside the stadiums each weekend. Their success was limited, as whilst they succeeded in preventing the supporters from going wild, the policemen were only able to concentrate on containing constant on-going riots. Increasing criticism was heard towards the police helplessness in eradicating the hooliganism phenomenon. A criticism, which naturally lowered the morale of the officers, involved. There are those who claim that this frustration by police officers reinforced rather than suppressed this football related violence.

Garry Armstrong, an anthropologist and a Sheffield United supporter, claims in his book Football Hooligans that police forces didn't only not suppress violent incidences, sometimes they even encouraged it. Supporters were sometimes forced to stand at the entrance to the ground, getting beaten up by police officers in full view of those passing by. One of the more familiar stories, known for it's brutality, Armstrong claims, is about a supporter who's hands were tied up and he was forced to run down the stand stairway, when only before he reached fence, his hands were untied and he could protect himself; if he made it.

The supporters, faces bloodied until they lost consciousness, were used as warning signs to other supporters. By the end of the seventies, these tactics were taken out of use, although policemen and supporters knew they were not completely abandoned. (Armstrong, 1998)

Years after this book was published, I heard from a steward at Stamford Bridge, the home stadium of the London club Chelsea, the following story: "Up until the nineties, the pitch was surrounded with a fence. Not just any fence, but an electric fence! Although it was never turned on during football matches, it was placed in order to prevent supporters from bursting to the pitch".

Armstrong keeps on elaborating about the enforcement of order. The presence of the police had a great effect on manifesting the 'disorder'. Police cars would rush out after the crowd leaving the stadium, causing a domino effect starting with a few hundred supporters running all around. This pursuit caused the cops to drive even faster, trying to stop the alleged hooligans.

Yet all of this is happening in a country that regards itself as the cultural centre of the civilised world. Football at that time was a game played at the kingdom's 'back yard'. This is the reason these horrible, violent sights could take place without threatening England's self-perception as a cultural, modern and rational empire. The football stadiums, some even until today, are located inside the neighbourhoods and are hidden by the residential houses. Foreigners who first come there will most likely have difficulty finding the place, even when it attracts thousands of supporters each week. League football matches were rarely broadcasted on television; Up until the sixties, the officials of the Football League bitterly objected to live broadcasting of the matches out of concern that the supporters might prefer watching the match from their living room couches rather than from inside the stadium. In the season of 1960/61 a first attempt was made to broadcast a live league match. The ITV network broadcasted the match between Blackpool and Bolton, and in this case also, only from the end of the first half. The broadcast was a flop and attracted harsh criticism, specifically regarding lack of interest, problematic photography and a very small audience in the stands (Imlach, 2005). A week later the network was supposed to broadcast a match between Arsenal and Newcastle, but Arsenal's board refused entry to the cameras. Following Arsenal, other clubs also refused to allow broadcasting of their matches, and the deal with the broadcasting network collapsed.

Up until the middle of the twentieth century, there was little connection between English football and European football. During the fifties, the English Football Association expressed a strong objection toward participating in European tournaments. The concern was that the load of matches would only damage the teams and the league. Additionally, until the end of the seventies, the English law prohibited participation of foreign players in the professional league. For all of these reasons, including hidden stadiums, forbidden TV broadcast and prevention from taking part in European competitions, made turning a blind eye on hooliganisms easier at that time.

The seventies brought along a new breeze of openness and continental cooperation in all areas, among which is football. British teams started playing in European competitions, foreign players join the local teams and live TV broadcast brought English matches to everywhere in the world. There and then, football changed from being a match played in England's "back-yard", into a match broadcasted on a wide screen in the guest room. Guests from every corner of the world are sitting in this guest room right now. That's why, from the moment the matches began, followed by the supporters violence, people calling for a dramatic change started being heard.

Wembley

The history of British football in the years in which it was considered a working class sport is full of stories of disasters and mismanagement. One of the first football disasters we know occurred in 1902, during a match between Scotland and England. At this stage rules of the game are not yet clear, and the system is not fixed. The English and Scottish players wear hats, because no one yet understands the potential of playing with the head. The English play individually: they take the ball and run towards the net. The Scottish embarrass the English national team by playing a yet unknown tactic: they move the ball from one player to another. While the game gradually develops on the grass, a wooden stand collapses and fatally buries twenty-five people beneath it. This is how the history of modern football in the UK begins, and so it will remain for almost ninety years ahead.

In 1923, Wembley Stadium in London was first opened. The first FA

Cup Final held in it was between Bolton Wanderers and West Ham United. One hundred thousand supporters were already standing in the stadium stands, whereas about a hundred thousand others are breaking in the stadium through the barriers, first to the stands, then to the pitch, increasing the number of spectators to a total of two hundred thousand. It is so crowded that it becomes hard to continue the match safely. Supporters are standing on the white lines, and each time the players have to take a corner kick, the match has to be delayed until the police are able to temporarily evacuate the area. At the end of the match Bolton Wanderers have won their first historical trophy, though people are beginning to realise that without further investment in facilities and proper management of supporters, dramatic disasters could occur. The first English football inquiry board is established.

Twenty years later, the overwhelmingly crowded matches are already a sight. Everyone knows that it is only a matter of time until a disaster takes place, yet what a great shock when it does occur. The year is 1946, and this is again within the framework of the FA Cup, this time in the quarter-final. Bolton Wanderers are playing against Stoke City, and eighty-five thousand spectators are crowded inside Burnden Park stadium, which, unluckily, is not able to handle this amount of people. The load on the Stands is so great that one of the supporting fences collapses and buries thirty-three supporters beneath it. England is shocked. A second inquiry committee is established.

Until 1971, three more disasters occurred in football stadiums around the country. Following each, an inquiry board is established, and five more recommendation reports are published. None of these reports brought about the desired change. In 1971, a shocking disaster strikes again, this time in Scotland. It is a nerve-wracking match between the country's top two teams, Rangers against Celtic taking place in Ibrox Stadium. The first eighty-nine minutes of the match passed without any goals. Suddenly, one minute before stoppage time Celtic score. The matter seemed closed, and the desperate Rangers supporters are starting to make their way out of the stadium. Somehow, in the final minute of the match, Rangers manage to score. Thousands of enthusiastic supporters standing on the stairs of gate 13 are now celebrating the unexpected goal. When someone fell on the stairs a chain reaction of people falling over them crushed sixty-six supporters to death, many of which were children. A Sixth inquiry board is established.

In time, disasters kept on occurring, inquiry committees are set up, but nothing brings about the desired change. The situation aggravates even further. Apart from the tragedies resulting from poor facilities, in the nineteen seventies English football had to deal with another equally frightening trouble: the local hooligan gangs that sought to make violence an integral part of the game. During the eighties, these threatening juvenile gangs started to accompany the teams to matches outside of England. All of these inflaming elements together create one of the most dramatic events to take place during 1985: the Heysel Stadium disaster in Brussels.

This was the Final of the European Cup between Liverpool and Juventus. Before the match, Liverpool supporters, some who were allegedly drunk, began to taunt the opposing club's supporters. Liverpool supporters broke into an area reserved for Juventus fans and the Italian supporters running away from the threat ran towards a concrete retaining wall. Fans already standing near the wall were crushed and eventually the wall collapsed. Many people climbed over the broken wall to safety, but many others were badly injured or died. The match was played in an attempt to prevent further violence, with Juventus winning 1–0. When the scale of the disaster become clear, the joy of the Italians was halted and thirty-nine bodies of supporters are evacuated from the ruins. The UEFA board decided to intervene and remove all English clubs from playing in European tournaments. True, the removal penalty is sweetened later, but the national pride of England suffers a fatal blow. The 'coal miners' have stained the white sofas of the great English civilization with black spots and something has to be done, but no one knows exactly what.

The Eighties are not easy years for the working class in England. At that time, the Prime Minister, Margaret Thatcher, adopts a revolutionary socio-economic policy, whereupon the main sources of income of blue-collar men, mainly coal miners, are shut down. Millions instantly become unemployed, and become solely dependent on welfare benefits from the

---

3. Taylor, L.J., (1990) The Hillsborough Stadium Disaster (15 April 1989). Final Report. London: HMSO.

state. The government's heavy hand does not skip the working class sport, while Thatcher and other politicians deal with denunciation of football supporters. The media is filled with quotations from members of parliament who condemned the phenomenon and those who take part in it. The result of this massive public condemnation is to antagonise the hooligan football citizens, and increase their social marginalisation. This way, they believed, it would be possible to reduce the phenomenon, perhaps even eradicate it. However, the denunciation system works like a boomerang and hooliganism is flourishing, fertilised by unemployment, frustration and a sense of class-consciousness. Three years after the Heysel Stadium disaster and another tragic disaster makes it clear that the lesson has not been learned.

In the year when Berlin Wall fell and Germany tries to convey a message of hope to the world, English football continues to face old problems. The FA Cup semi-final between Liverpool and Nottingham Forest is held at Hillsborough Stadium in Sheffield. Liverpool supporters arrive in their masses, some delay due to heavy traffic, creating massive pressure on the gates of the stadium. The pressure is so great that the local police in a reckless decision allow free entry to the venue from one of the gates. The entrance of the enthusiastic crowd of supporters to an already packed stand, causes crushing of supporters who are standing close to the pitch, near the fences.

Maybe some of the supporters who were crushed could have been saved if the police allowed the opening of the fences and an entrance to the pitch. But in those years the football match is considered paramount, and in order not to interfere with the match, the police physically detained desperate attempts to escape from the dangerous balcony. Ninety-five Liverpool supporters died as a result of this terrible incident with another injured fan dying four years later. Those who come to Anfield stadium nowadays, face an enormous shocking memorial monument. On my last visit in the stadium, over nineteen years after the disaster, I witnessed many people who still come to the cold tombstone, carrying fresh flower bouquets in their hands.

The reason the Heysel Stadium disaster and Hillsborough are engraved in the collective memory of every football supporter in the world, while other disasters have vanished from the pages of history, is that in the years in which they occur, English football was revealed to Europe and the rest of the world. The media reached everywhere; football stories reach every ear, leaving the United Kingdom ashamed. the local bubble burst open and can no longer treat the football match as a naughty child who is acting up a bit. Football is now a massive entertainer for millions who lay back in the virtual royalty guestroom, and in here, no swearing, hitting or throwing dirt on the floor is allowed.

International Football

And there goes the wild child, out of his home boundaries, making a riot in the entire neighbourhood; In addition to the hooliganism spreading around the English football clubs, during the seventies, the phenomenon now follows England's national team. Until this time, only a small amount of supporters would accompany England's team beyond the borders of the United Kingdom.

Starting the early seventies of the twentieth century, violence among English football supporters was a common sight. In 1977, twenty thousand supporters made their way with the team to the little Kingdom of Luxembourg. Hundreds of policeman and soldiers are set to 'welcome' them there. The visitors however, are not afraid, and violently clash with local supporters and the police until blood is spilled. England is humiliated. Local politicians are taking advantage of every platform to condemn the phenomenon. 'Animals', one called them, while others argue that this is a flattering nickname, as 'no animals behave so horribly.'

Three years later, during the European Championship Cup match in Italy, the English supporters tangle again. When arriving Italy, enthusiastic local supporters who are ready for battle await them there. The police arrested many England supporters, although some of the arrests are for protective reasons, saving them from the hands of local supporters. Violent pictures are again released to the world and England is again, embarrassed. Prime Minister Thatcher calls the violent supporters 'disgrace'. In one documentary interview The Real Football Factory, which monitors the phenomenon, an ex-hooligans tells: 'Everyone called us a disgrace. Shame. We decided that if now we put the country to shame, we'll show them what a shame we could be. It was a start of an internal war between us and those who are slandering us. Their calls only encouraged us to go on'.

Until the mid-eighties supporters who follow the national team to European tournaments are mostly supporters of lower league clubs. Those supporters had limited opportunities to follow their team to away games in Europe, so they found in the national team tours an opportunity to experience something new. In 1985 however, following the Heysel Stadium disaster, all of the English clubs are punished with exclusion from all European competitions. The national team, however, continues to participate in European and international frameworks as before, and now it is a magnet for supporters of all football clubs in the country.

To the 1988 European Football Championship held in Germany tens thousands of supporters had already arrived. This time it is not just supporters of small clubs, but supporters of all clubs in England, young and old, gathering into a shared experience of an away match. The English supporters, who are known by their names and reputations, are accepted by their German hosts who are armed with batons and tear gas. The local police decided not to intervene, laying the foundation for the most violent twenty-four hours in the history of England supporters' away games.

The Euro matches of 1990 are held in Italy. Under the influence of the riots in Germany from two years before, and following the Hillsborough disaster which occurred one year earlier, Italy has prepared itself for the English supporters with an exceptionally large police force – seven thousands policemen. Preparations for football matches against the England national team looked like preparations for a military battle. Three years later, in Rotterdam, the English supporters await the biggest gang seen so far: four thousand local supporters eager to fight. English hooligans benefit from the development; a local phenomenon that began in their home has now reached the most important city centres in Europe. All are playing their game according to their English rules, and the world becomes one big playground. In their country, disapproval continues regarding them and their behaviour, but the condemnation only contributes to their motivation rather than depresses it. The circle of repeating violence-condemnation-violence overwhelms the decision-makers in England, and they always end up helpless. England realises only too late that condemnation of the phenomenon and suppressing it only manages to increase the motivation for violence, thus making it even more widespread, so it decides to change strategy.

The Taylor Report

England is highly concerned about the way it is perceived by others. It likes to think of itself as enlightened, moral and civilised. The British admire their House of Lords, worship the Queen and believe that if there is a God, it must reside between Victoria Street and Hyde Park. 'Britishness' is all about going to museums, high-class restaurants and Shakespeare's plays in the West End. It is a tradition, a vast literature and a nation of gentlemen bowing in front of ladies, inviting them to dance in the grand ballroom. Suddenly, football comes and destroys everything. Up until then the social hierarchy could be blamed and the game of football could be associated to workers. Upper class women could ask in wonder: 'Am I the wife of a coal miner?' And leave it at that; to allow mobs to vent their feelings of frustration in small local football stadiums, far from the public, national and international eye. Nevertheless, from the moment violent supporters come across every corner in Europe and television started showing the horrifying pictures to the world, then those who are not residents of England begin calling them all 'violent Englishmen'. Gentle-manners are replaced by tattooed young men, exposing their white beer bellies while couples dancing are replaced by fists and juicy curses. England cannot live with that.

The Hillsborough disaster in the late eighties that led to the unnecessary deaths of ninety-six football supporters, made it clear that this cannot continue. The government orders the establishment of a special inquiry committee lead by Judge Peter Taylor. Taylor's committee report was published in two phases; a brief, sixty pages long report was published in the first phase, offering forty-three specific recommendations, twenty-eight of them for immediate implementation. The second, more thorough part of the report, includes one hundred and eighteen pages and offers substantial change of the game. Judge Taylor is recommending that the proposed measures required to ensure the safety of spectators at matches is just not enough; what is needed here is the vision and imagination to achieve new ethos to the game of football.

The concept guiding the Taylor Commission report is simple: If we treat football supporters as savages, that is how they would behave. But if we treat them as civilised human beings, they will begin to see themselves as such. Simple as it may sound, this statement is completely contrary to the spirit in which it was customary to refer to football supporters until then. In his report Judge Taylor criticises all match-related directors, including the police. He argues that the experience of watching a football match today is reminiscent of the experience of going into battle. Supporters are being confined behind high fences as if they were in prison. They are considered criminals before even committing an offence and so they are treated. Because they are already outlaws in the eyes of society, it's easier for them to commit a future offence. The experience of being a fan at an away match is even more intimidating. A limited number of supporters surrounded by dozens of policemen, sometimes reinforced with dogs, watching every step they make; from the moment they get off the bus or leave the train station. After the match, they are kept for thirty minutes in the stands. They are football supporters, not prisoners.

According to the recommendation of the judge Taylor, all the country's stadiums were renovated in the following years and the fan terracing progressively became seating only grandstands. The fence separating the supporters from the pitch are removed, reduced number of police officers are replaced with unarmed security guards. On duty police are out the viewer's sight, they sit in a small capsule above one of the stands. From this small room, they monitor dozens of screens that transmit live images of hundreds of security cameras from any point outside and inside the stadium. They are able to point out any suspicious persons among the forty to sixty thousand spectators at any time, if necessary.

Even the match experience is changed. The committee's report does not omit any element, large or small, of the football experience, and recommends making changes in each and every function the stadium has to offer. It is desirable that the event organisers offer entertainment preceding the match; it will attract more supporters to arrive early to the venue and will thus spare the long lines at the entrance. Public restrooms should be installed for both men and women in sufficient quantity. The food offered in the stands is recommended to be varied, healthy and hygienic. Rubbish bins must be placed in as many places as possible. TV screens at the entrance to the stands will provide the supporters with results from other stadiums. Rubber flooring will prevent slipping and will conceal the accumulated rubbish and so on. A positive atmosphere will be the one to restore pride to the English football game.

The Taylor Commission report severely criticised the management of the Football League (FL) and the Football Association (FA). Their only concern was to keep the match on the pitch going. So they chose to isolate the pitch from the supporters with high fences, and ordered the continuance of the matches even when there were disasters happening in the stands. As a result of this terrible misjudgement, they did not open the gates that separated the pitch from the crowd at the Hillsborough stadium, and nearly a hundred supporters were crushed to their death. Taylor Commission report recommended that;

The safety of the supporters should be the primary source of concern to the managements, and clearly make sure to prefer this consideration over any other. Two years after the report was published, the league management is replaced and a new league is established. The Premier League.

The English National team matches also change. In 1996 England is ready to regain its injured pride and hosts the Euro tournament entitled 'Football comes home'. This is a great time to host the European Championship, because in the wake of the report's recommendations most football stadiums in the country have been renovated, and England shows Europe and the world the highest level possible of stadiums and sports facilities. The media joins the national mission and announces the world about football culture's rebirth. England is again a culture and a civilisation. Football is the national game, and its gift to the world.

Four years later, it's the first year of the new millennium, and the European Cup tournament is co-hosted by two countries – the Netherlands and Belgium. Ten years after the publication of the Taylor report, England's status, at least in terms of football, inspires optimism but still requires proof. It's like a little kid knows he made nonsense before, and now he claims he had grown up. England is determined to show the world that it's fans infantile behaviour during the seventies and eighties remains in the past.

It is not so successful. Like supporters from all over Europe, Masses of England supporters arrive to the city centres of both host countries. The

English team competes in group A. Most supporters are concentrated in the city of Charleroi, Belgium. Their reception by the local police is very suspicious. Police and army forces are waiting with water cannons down in the town squares, ready to go into action first when conflict breaks out. Stress takes its toll, and confrontations are next in line. Water cannons are activated, and military transport vehicles occupy urban plazas as if it were in the middle of a war, overriding the festive atmosphere. Many are relieved that the English team fails to qualify for the next stage, and the supporters go home disappointed after only three matches. But that's not the whole story.

While police and army forces are engaged in riots in city centres in Belgium, the Dutch police are trying a different tactic. No armed police walking around on foot in the squares, rather they are assimilated peacefully in the audience. They are joking with the supporters, and give out black police hats to many of them. There are no two opposing sides seeking a violent confrontation in this festival. With a police hat on their heads, the behaviour of the supporters during and after the matches is surprisingly peaceful. Although France won the tournament and took the championship, the whole of Europe has benefited from the experience. The Euro 2000 tournament, with its unique structure, provides an instructive example of the arguments that led Judge Taylor in his report ten years earlier; if we treat football supporters as criminals, that is how they would behave. But if we treat them as civilized human beings, they will begin to see themselves as such.

And that's about it. Excluding some exceptional minor events, in all the following tournaments the English supporters were praised for their behaviour: the 2002 World Cup in Japan as well as in Euro 2004 in Portugal. Even the 2006 World Cup match in Germany, where English supporters previously showed the most violent hooliganism, pass pleasantly. Although the English team crowned biggest underdog of these tournaments, the reason is football. And that's what matters.

Chelsea

The transformation football went through in the past decades – from being a game played by children of nobility in Public Schools to a working class sport, from a violent, vulgar game to a popular cultural entertainment, as well as the big change in the British football supporters behaviour, show the British nature in neither good or bad and it doesn't have a genetic stamp determining the civilians innate behaviour. This proves that it's not that the football match itself encourages violence, as sometimes claimed by the game's objectors. Football matches in England and around the world are what people make of them, and the supporters behave as accordingly. While this is a slow and gradual process, football's sympathy can let go of its negative aspects such as violence and vandalism and acquire itself some Western cultural traits.

I remember watching a football match in April 2007, at the Stamford Bridge stadium, the home ground of Chelsea Football Club. My ticket was in the Bolton visiting team grandstand. Some supporters made their way from Bolton to London, but most seats beside me were empty. This match is especially important to Chelsea, which still has a small chance to compete against Manchester United in the championship. Two young English men, wearing Chelsea's blue shirts, arrive fifteen minutes after the start of the match and take their seat next to us. Although they are young, as can be seen on their faces, they are pretty large physically. Earrings in different sizes are decorating their faces and their bodies are painted with tattoos. I'm a little worried. Stadiums usually take care of sealed separation between supporters of different clubs. A couple of Bolton supporters around me notice the two uninvited guests, they do not seem pleased. The air is heating up; both blue supporters take a Chelsea flag out of their bag and approach to hang it on the closest stand. A Bolton fan throws them a word. They do not respond. A young security guard comes close. She is about five feet tall, her body is petite and her voice is high, almost childish.

She asks both Chelsea's supporters to show her their tickets. They pull them out of their pockets with a sheepish look on their faces. The security guard is gone for a few minutes. Meanwhile, Chelsea scores and takes the lead 2–1 against Bolton. The electronic scoreboard shows the unbelievable result from their rivals match: Everton 2, Manchester United 0. If the result remains the same, Chelsea is back in the fight for the championship. All Chelsea supporters stand up and shout with joy. All but two of our supporters in the stands, who are now engaged in conversation with the security guard.

"I apologise, your tickets are fake."

"We bought them outside, but we paid full price," says one of them.

"I ask you to move and sit in the stands with the rest of your team's supporters."

"We tried, but there is no vacant seats."

"I apologize. In this case you will be asked to leave the match. You must respect the supporters of Bolton."

Chelsea are one goal ahead, Manchester United are two behind. It could be a dramatic match, which will be remembered forever in the history books of English football. Will the two devoted supporters pass the opportunity to take part in history?

In one unexpected moment, the two supporters in blue get up from their seats, show off their tattoos and look even more intimidating and. leave the stand. Quietly, peacefully, without saying a word. The security guard escorts them out, and says goodbye once they leave the stadium.

Sixty minutes later, Bolton recover and draw. Manchester United beat Everton after an impressive reversal and wins season's championship. I'm sitting in the visitors' stands, a bit overwhelmed by all the drama in the match, especially by the two local supporters in the visitors' stand. I think to myself that almost nothing is left from the English football game as it was by the end of the twentieth century.

Being a fan of a Premier League club from the end of the twentieth century

Civilisation

Norbert Elias was one of the most important sociologists of the last century. His most important work is the eight hundred pages long book called The Civilising Process in which he examines the transformation process of European civilisation, as we know it today. In the centre of the book Elias makes a claim that civilising is essentially a process of refinement. Certain behaviours that in the past were customarily carried out in public, stop being legitimate and are moved to society's backstage. The book is filled with examples, most of which are taken from norms around the dining table.

Until the sixteenth century, says Elias, the French and Germans would eat their meals using their hands. Peasants as well as nobility would poke their fingers deep into the meat served at the table and pull out the piece their heart desired. Forks were not used and rules of hygiene are a much later invention. Dead animals were brought whole to the table. "Not only whole fish and whole birds (sometimes with their feathers) but also whole rabbits, lambs, and quarters of veal appear on the table, not to mention the larger venison or the pigs and oxen roasted on the spit," Elias details. Making the animal edible was done for all to see. Even the way guests would behave at the table probably would have caused us nowadays to skip the meal. Spitting and breaking wind were commonplace and blowing one's nose was done with two fingers of the left hand, with the remnants of the snot discarded on the table or floor.

You'd think the scientific discoveries regarding bacteria and diseases caused by pollution are the ones that led to the sharp increase in demand for hygiene, but Elias argues otherwise. In his opinion, the European nobility's attempt to distinguish itself from the masses is the cause for the slow refinement process. At some point, the middle and lower classes, who aspired to be like nobility, also adopted the new conduct. Historically, medical discoveries were much later than these changes in behaviour, proving that what prompted the change was a social process and not a scientific one. The new western rules required much more work in the kitchen. They began cutting the meat and processing it in the kitchen, away from the diner's eye, until it lost the shape of the animal it was.

Breaking wind was allowed only behind closed doors, and for nose wiping and spitting, handkerchiefs were invented, they had become a must item for any Western nobleman. Using a cloth to hide one's necessities is also compatible with the definition of Elias process of civilising: the transfer of shameful behaviour behind the scenes of social life. One of the ways in which the courtly aristocratic society used to educate young men new ways of proper behaviour was publishing books on manners for whoever could read and write in the country's Public Schools. For example, in the book De civilitate morum puerilium (A Handbook on Good Manners for Children) by Erasmus (France, 1530): 'It's just as rude to lick greasy fingers as it is to wipe them on your clothing, Use a cloth or napkin instead.' 'Some people, no sooner than they've sat down, immediately stick their hands into the dishes of food. This is the manner of wolves.' 'Making a raucous noise or shrieking intentionally when you sneeze, or showing off by carrying on sneezing on purpose, is very ill-mannered.' 'To fidget around in your seat, and to settle first on one buttock and then the next, gives the impression that you are repeatedly farting, or trying to fart.' Education is the most effective way to encourage change in behaviour.

The shock felt in England during the eighties in the face of violent behaviour in football stadiums is reminiscent of the disgust we had from hearing descriptions of the past European behaviours, which Elias describes in his book. As we would certainly be embarrassed to sit at a large dining table during the fifteenth century, when twenty diners use the tablecloth to wipe their nose and remove mucus from the bodies, so were the upper classes in England while watching football matches dominated by a cursing and kicking hooligan mob. When English football was opened to the world during the seventies, and violence in football began to be in the centre of public attention, governmental authorities sought to hide it, as if it does not exist.

Sport is considered a way to unload, that's why no one believed it would be possible to completely eliminate violence from the stadiums. Football is a rough game, which encourages an emotional outburst. But is there a way of controlling the physical and mental excitement the match generates, so the next step – translation of that excitement act into violence – will be prevented? Is it possible to not only hide that kind behaviour, but to eradicate it altogether? Norbert Elias talks about the spitting in public phenomenon, which was common in Europe until the seventeenth century. Until then, it was regarded as a natural action that could not be avoided, such as blowing your nose. Therefore, the process of civilising with regard to this act required only to hide your secretions behind a handkerchief cloth, but not to avoid it. Avoiding it is considered harmful to the body. But as time passed, spitting became less common, until it disappeared almost entirely amongst Western behaviour. People rarely spit at all, they can avoid doing so for many hours every day.

So in football until the nineties, England was saturated with hooliganism and violence inside and outside the stadiums. The justification for this was also physical; playing football, it is argued, is an exciting sensory experience altogether. The excitement of the match is then easily translated into violence off the field.

Functionalist theories talked about the human body as a perfect system that knows how to release pressure, which is the result of daily life, through safe activities such as football. Meaning, during football matches the body unloads natural urges of violence, so that it could return to its calm and cultural behaviour. Therefore, supporter's violence is only natural, healthy and necessary.

Over the years however, the game has become so elitist in England so that today, even verbal abuse are considered a deviation. English football matches have become such a sterile cultural experience, evident by Johnny's apology to me for the violent language that was used by that granddaddy who sat next to us at the Emirates Stadium. The process of civilising that football is going through in recent years seem to do more than just conceal the supporters violent behaviour; it manages to almost completely eliminate it by turning it unacceptable. The process is driven and empowered by the management of the Premier League and football clubs in the country, who seek to create a warm, embracing atmosphere, cultural and caring, that will flatter and support the supporters. They do it by careful creating league matches and creating intimacy between the player and the supporter, watching the match at the stadium, in a pub or even from home. Another important tool in this social change is the educational process children undergo in football academies. I will deal with these issues in the following chapters.

Emirates Stadium

Time passed, seasons changed and I went on spending the weekends at Premier League matches. During one of my visits to the Emirates Stadium, a League Cup match takes place. Arsenal are hosting Newcastle United. Match tickets are sold at relatively affordable prices. A few minutes before kick-off, the crowd begins to settle in their places to the sound of soothing songs played by the perfect Emirates sound system. Song after song, no clear order between them. The song that is playing next begins with a loud trumpet cheer. King Elvis' soft voice follows, humming an emotional "uh uhuh".

Since the beginning of my work in London and the first match I went to with Johnny, I got to watch quite a few Arsenal matches at the Emirates Stadium. My initial amazement at the round monster, into which sixty thousand spectators enter in a matter of minutes, has not faded since. The long corridors, bright lights and luxurious, perfectly polished ladies restroom, still take my breath away for a moment today. I still remember the feeling of a forced experience, staged, organised to the last detail; an experience deprived of all the spontaneity we can imagine exists at a football match. One of the things that captivated me at first was the songs played in the stadium. Back then, the organisers chose to play Robbie Williams's Let me entertain you. Now they play The Wonder of you by Elvis. Some of its words are:

When no one else can understand me
when everything I do is wrong
you give me hope and consolation

you give me strength to carry on…

As in school literature classes, I ask myself: Who is the speaker? Who is the recipient? Is Arsenal the one that sometimes succeeds, occasionally has difficulties, and now seeks to thank all tens of thousands of its supporters who escort them all along the way, give it hope, comfort and strength to move on? Indeed lovely.

To be honest, my job is pretty boring. While everyone is having fun, I'm concerned with the question 'what makes them enjoy'. When supporters take pleasure from a goal, I am busy checking the resolution of the images projected on the giant screens and how often they play a rerun of the goal. I'm more tied up with the production process of playing football than with the actual match on the pitch. My purpose here is to understand the song selection, the food sold in the buffet, the videos projected on the screens, the role of announcer. So, yes, I could have worked in far worse conditions, live in a remote village, eat strange food and accompanying the local natives to the hunting fields. Elvis goes on with his love song:

And you're always there
to lend a hand in everything I do
that's the wonder, the wonder of you…

There is no doubt; Arsenal supporters are always there. In league matches, European Cups, and even today, when this is 'only' a League Cup match. Sixty thousand seats are all taken as always, even though match tickets were sold separately from the season ticket. It is the supporters who pay tens of pounds to watch the match, making Arsenal one of the most profitable clubs in Premier League. Their contribution, however goes far beyond money.

The vibe in the stadium is amazing. People have already taken their place in the stands while enjoying the act of courting the masses. Like in an Bollywood movies, where the girl at one time hides behind a tree while her lover sings her a love song, and when she comes out of her hiding, he hides behind a tree, letting her hum her love song for him. This is an act of flirtation that draws sixty thousand people to a dance with no one particularly taking the lead.

And when you smile, the world brighter
You touch my hand and I'm king

Your kiss is worth a fortune

Your love for me is everything

I could go on with the martyred attitude I adopted for myself in my first few weeks here. "I'm here to work, not to enjoy". "When everyone is enjoying the experience, I examine it in depth". But I will not lie; I find myself having a lot of fun when I visit the Emirates Stadium. I enjoy the feeling of a social event that accompanies the walk through the corridors. I love the fancy outfits and the casual chitchats on matters of utmost importance; I take pleasure with the quiet polite speech, and politely embarrassed whenever a gentleman holds the door for a moment for me to pass.

Perhaps it is human nature: We get used to good things too quickly. And from the moment we were invited to sit around the table at the gourmet restaurant, it will be difficult for us to go back to eating fast food from street stalls. I've never been to the Highbury Stadium. They say it might have been a sacred place, mythological. At first glance Arsenal's new home seemed like a huge glass monster, though after sitting in its comfortable seats and tasting its delicacies, you discover that sometimes a monster could be nice.

It's almost seven. A short break of words in favour of the repeating "uuhh"… Elvis is ready for show's highlight; a short drum solo and he continues:

I guess, I'll never know

the reason why you love me like you do

that's the wonder, the wonder of you.

As soon as he finishes pronouncing these words, in perfect timing, there come the players in red out of the tunnel. Suddenly everything is clear: Arsenal's players are themselves the wonder. They are the object of love. They are the ones always there to encourage us, their touch makes us kings. The subject of courtship has emerged from behind the imaginary Bollywood tree, and sixty thousand supporters, backed by the King, singing with one voice to the red eleven: that's the wonder, wonder in you, enjoying the public act of love, and yet – felt so intimate.

So, yes, I understand that the intimate feelings shared by tens thousands of supporters with their club are dictated and executed perfectly by someone behind the scenes. Nevertheless, I enjoy the experience so much at the moment that I forget all about the production processes and get addicted for one moment, along with everyone else, to the wonder, the wonder in you.

Behind the scenes

Since the early nineties, when the conclusions of the Taylor report began to be implemented, the stadiums in England underwent a dramatic change. The metal fences were removed, and the distance between the audience sitting in the stands and the players on the pitch got shorter. Surprisingly, this didn't cause an increase in the illegal invasion of supporters onto the pitches. Not threatening and unarmed security guards have replaced the police, who use to use force to block passage between the stand and the pitch. Architect designed stadiums saw it as a goal to give viewers a sense of proximity to what happens on the pitch. So, no matter where you sit at Stamford Bridge, you'll always feel like Frank Lampard takes the free-kick from the corner, right here next to your water bottle. In the Emirates Stadium, you can see every movement made by manager Arsene Wenger, every twitch in the face of the goalie. Giant screens will broadcast the parts missed if you were too hung up with the pie in your hands or if you went to buy a drink. This experience is just for you, at least so they manage to convince you.

The feeling the supporters have the ability to touch the players exist in moments when a match is being held on the pitch as well as in moments it seems nothing is going on. The football club's public relations departments invests a lot of imagination and energy think of ways to connect the supporters to their admired players. Particularly in recent years, when the players have massively grown apart from the social status of their supporters. They do it in different ways, including selling all kinds of printed merchandise with the club's crest, surrounding the supporter from the moment he opens his eyes (on a Arsenal/Chelsea/Manchester United/Liverpool's pillow), drinks coffee (in the club's mug), drives to work (sitting on a seat with the club's crest printed on it), going to a football match after work (wearing the club's shirt, what else), take a shower and drying off with a towel (you already know the drill) and finally goes to sleep on the club's pillow (I skipped the underwear part. You are welcome to use your imagination). The supporters being able to buy and wear their favourite players shirts lets them feel 'as one' with them, or at least make them feel closer. If not in reality, at least in fantasy, which in this case, has a strong impact.

The club's products are not the only way. When no football match is on, organised groups tours are held in the stadiums about five times a day. The tour guides try not only to show people the magnificent stadium, but also to generate a sense of pride and intimacy between the club and its supporters.

The highlight of these tours is the visit in the team players dressing rooms. The tour guide sat us on comfortable leather, elliptical shaped, seats in the Gunners' dressing room. The players sit in the same seats for each match.

"You!" the guide called to one of the children, "You're sitting right where Emmanuel Adebayor sat this week. And you ..." He pointed to the kid to his left, "are sitting in the usual place of the goalkeeper, Jens Lehmann."

Chelsea's dressing room is less impressive than that of the Gunners in the Emirates, but its entrance is more exciting especially because a shirt of each of the players is hung on each of their lockers. On the left you can see the shirts of John Terry, Frank Lampard and Joe Cole. The shirts hanging on the right belong to Michael Ballack and Andrey Shevchenko. You can imagine the few hours before an important match, when players come to find their kits just as they are now, lying clean and fresh, waiting to be worn. To make them feel even closer, the guide opens the lockers to show, "what does a professional player's locker looks like?" "A picture of himself, of course. What kind of player doesn't love himself?" "He has a tape and extra boot studs. Each player usually brings three to six pairs of boots to every match. He will pick what boots to play in before the match." At that moment you could almost smell the player's anxiety in the prematch, their energy at half-time and their sweat at the end of ninety minutes. Even if you just imagine that you can smell it, it's still smell wonderful.

The media also has a part in creating an almost personal connection between players and their supporters. In recent years, TV broadcasts around the world went through a significant change in the way they shoot football matches; moving to close-up shots and focusing in the players personal stories during the match. Today, television camera enters intimate situations that belonged previously to the football players only.

One night, Johnny and I were watching a Liverpool match in one of the pubs in north London. The big pitch is seen on the giant screen just as the players return from half-time. Liverpool's players are standing there, waiting for the other team's players to come out. The camera focuses on number eight, Steven Gerrard, the team's captain. He scratches his neck. You can see that something was bothering him. Maybe a little sore, maybe something on his shirt? Liverpool supporters are a little worried. After a moment it goes away and the supporters relax. The ability to feel so close to the players until you notice even the smallest details in their behaviour, gives us a sense of being a part of the match. As the players status grows farther away from their supporters, so does the camera becomes closer, trying to close the gap and prevent the alienation that could occur between the two.

Web sites, computer games and the club's official products such as books and DVDs, appear every season in recent years. They work in a similar way. Many websites allow you 'to be the coach', and play with 'your players'. On PlayStation you are actually 'them', running, kicking, sweating.

Biographies and autobiographies have become popular too, and readers are invited to enter the players, coaches and team owners' private lives. Bookstores have many books dedicated just to football. The football book industry in recent years has received an unprecedented momentum, which is relatively rare in sports. Here is an example of a relatively old biography of Wayne Rooney written at a time when he played for Everton. The book was written by Harry Harris and Danny Polebrook, in two hundred and seventeen pages, the authors write about every detail of his life.

Graham, Wayne's younger brother, was an aspiring boxer. Rooney, according to the book, had no desire for the glamour of football life in England; He prefers to spend his afternoons kicking balls with his friends from the neighbourhood. He wears football jerseys instead of suits and plays Sony PlayStation instead of attending glamorous parties. The authors turn Rooney from a football player who earns millions into a living human figure that each of us could imagine meeting in the grocery store. From being a legendary figure, he is made accessible, from being divine; he is suddenly the boy next door.

In David Beckham's autobiography, which was written when he made the well-publicised move from Manchester United to Real Madrid, he tells in the first person about his way to the top. He writes about his father who dreamed of being a footballer himself, but when he grew up and realised he could no longer fulfil his dream, gave up everything to train his talented son; he writes about the long training hours, beginning from the end of the school day until late darkness, and about the insistence that he go to church every Sunday, so that little David could play in its amateur league. The book is packed with pictures of the star; since his childhood up to his transfer to Spain. Beckham talks about the relationship with his wife Victoria, and his love for the little ones. One image, particularly intimate, shows father David's bare feet beside his two young sons while three of them are lying in bed. You cannot get any closer than that.

Hundreds of biographies and autobiographies of this kind have been written thus far. The simplest and most immediate reason for the phenomenon is, of course – money. As predicted, most books offer basic knowledge. They were written in the heat of the moment, in order to catch the wave of popularity at the time. The book by Harris and Polebrook, which was published in 2003, intended to glorify Wayne Rooney's decision to stay in Everton forever. Then again, the book became irrelevant as soon as Rooney signed a contract with Manchester United. Now it can be moved to the clearance bookshelf.

Beyond the simple explanation in the form of coloured notes with the scowling face of the Queen, these life stories have another effect. They help revive and bring closer those football players who dramatically grew apart from their supporters in recent years; they make young children imagine themselves kicking balls at a wall in Merseyside with Wayne Rooney. Slightly older children can find similarities between their life story and that of Cristiano Ronaldo, whereas fans of David Beckham can now imagine how he looks in bed. All of these create a sense of intimacy between supporters and players, even when the supporters do not physically come to encourage their team in the stadium. Even if that feeling of intimacy is one sided, or just a figment of their imagination, unlike the one existing between a supporter and his team players at the end of the last century, it's still there, anyway you look at it. So, true, you are no more likely to run into your favourite player at the grocery store, and the chances of sharing a drink with him in one of the local pubs are not particularly high, nevertheless, football has become an intimate experience nowadays. It was not taken from anyone. On the contrary, it was given to us as a gift in a way we could never imagine possible fifty years ago.

The beautiful game

The change in the games status is reflected in money, lots of money. If in the seventies, you could get a ticket to watch a match at a cost of up to one pound, today, a basic ticket to a Premier League match costs around forty to fifty pounds, in case you're lucky enough to get a ticket. Demand for tickets is high, and some of the major clubs don't even release single tickets for sale. Even purchasing a season ticket is not a simple undertaking, with the major clubs in the Premier League having a long waiting list, often comprised of tens of thousands of pending season ticket holders. Clubs allow 'senior' subscribers to renew their subscription every season.

"On the last check we made, we found some supporters who are more than a hundred and thirty years old", one of the Arsenal's tour guides told me once. "We asked a bit and found that even when our supporters die, their children do not inform us, but renew the subscription on their behalf, to circumvent the forty thousand people on the waiting list. An Arsenal season ticket has become a property inherited from father to son."

The high demand leads to a thriving black market for ticket at outrageous prices ranging from two hundred fifty to five hundred pounds for a single ticket. There is a section in the Arsenal's Emirates Stadium called 'The diamond', which is only one level less luxurious than the private booths. This grandstand subscription can be purchased for twenty-five thousand pounds a season, where the buyers are obligated to purchase a subscription for thirty-five years. Therefore, the transaction amounts for one seat comes down to almost a million pounds per one seat.

"We thought there would be no demand for these seats. We were surprised by the amount of people who asked for them: Give us the best seats you have!" so they say at Arsenal.

In order to watch the match from a private booth, Chelsea supporters, mostly private companies will have to say goodbye to one million pounds each season. The acquisition contract of this private booth is for ten years in advance so that the overall transaction sums up in around ten million pounds per one booth.

The big clubs have another department named the 'hospitality department'. The role of this department is to entertain supporters who are interested in a few hours of pampering in the stadium at the day of the match. The lucky supporters get to enjoy fine food, good seats and a grand tour in the stadium. All this for the 'modest' amount of two to five hundred pounds for a single match.

Selling season tickets is not the only fiscal pump, it's not the biggest too. A large amount of money enters the clubs from sponsors. Some companies are willing to pay big bucks so that their name will be shown on the big screens or having their logo displayed on the stadium walls. The clubs pick these companies carefully. When a certain publishing agreement is approved, it will bring the club a profit of no less than half a million pounds per season. Adidas, the official sponsor of Chelsea FC, pays the club a hundred and twenty million pounds to appear behind the manager while he gives an interview, and to be the only company selling the clubs official shirts. Samsung pays a relatively paltry amount, 'only' fifty-five million pounds for its logo to appear on those same shirts.

A few decades earlier, during the middle of the twentieth century football clubs were striving for sponsors, paying for kits and travelling fee. Very rarely a company agreed to donate money for that purpose, as they didn't want to be linked with the game of football. Things have certainly changed since then.

The improvement in football's social status is not only expressed in the big money that goes in and out of the clubs in recent years. It is also reflected in changing the way the game is played and perceived in the eyes of its audience. Later I will show how the football game itself has changed during the past fifty years, by comparing of the FA Cup Final match in 1957 to the Cup Final match in 2007. I will only briefly mention here that the change in the game began in the early nineties, when the Premier League was officially opened. The emphasis was on the way the game is played, rather than focusing only on the question of the result, as in the past. Questions about the quality of the game and the shape became more significant, and the demand for a 'beautiful game' was made more frequent and demanding. To some extent, the football game has become a somewhat artistic activity, where the game's result, which is undoubtedly its primary objective, is forced to coexist with criteria such as aesthetics and virtuoso performances.

In 1999, Arsene Wenger, the coach of Arsenal said; "There is no disgrace in wanting to win, but it has to be done – the right way – within the spirit of football". Wenger asked to emphasise the quality of the game, the performance of the players on the pitch, the grace. That's why even though his list of achievements is not as impressive as that of his competitors, during the seasons in which he manage the north London exalted club, he is still considered an idol of football supporters worldwide.

The demand for 'beautiful football' is not exclusive to Arsenal. More and more club owners are asking their team to play 'beautiful football', exciting football. At Chelsea, for example, the issue of this beautiful game was the cause of the frequent firing of managers. The concept of football as a type of art form is somehow consistent with the grasp of the game as an aristocratic activity, as a game for gentlemen, knights and royal courtiers. If you wish for the high class to choose football as a pastime worthy of their leisure, it is essential to make sure the game will include characteristics that will flatter their social status, such as beauty, gentle-manners and a noble spirit. To paraphrase Norbert Elias's doctrine mentioned here previously: when inviting high-class people to a meal, one should make sure that the table is set with a plate, a knife and a fork.

Football knights

Maybe the most significant expression of England's ruling status towards the game   is reflected in the decision to grant nobility titles to football players and managers. In the feudal times royal ranks were inherited or given only to those whose land was large enough to impress the royal family. Nowadays, titles are divided according to what the royalty calls: 'Actions, achievements and special services', made in favour of the state and the Queen.

Throughout most of the twentieth century rarely were football players honoured with a royal rank. In 1927, John Charles Clegg was given the title 'knight'. Clegg is considered the first player honoured with a degree of knighthood. Although in the letter describing the reasons for granting the honourable title, football was never mentioned. This is not surprising given that football was a working class sport, nor a profession honoured by the Monarch.

Throughout the next thirty years, no more footballers were honoured with a title. The sixties were a little more successful in that sense. In 1965, the player Stanley Matthews who played with Stoke City and Blackpool, was named 'Knight'. Matthews was chosen as the first 'European Player of the Year' and kept playing professional football until he reached the age of fifty. Knowledgeable sources say that he was the best dribbler of all times. Two years later, the England team's manager, Alf Ramsey won the same honour following the winning by England of the World Championship, an achievement that has not been repeated since. Again, two years later, the manager of Manchester United became Sir Matt Busby following his club winning the European Cup that year. It's not surprising that the three dignitaries, who won the royal titles during the sixties, received them due to their successes in Europe as well as around the world. England, as stated, is very sensitive to the way in which it is perceived abroad.

The seventies and eighties saw no titles of nobility granted to football players, which is not that surprising, given the violence and negative stigma of the game at that time. Only towards the end of that century, following changes to the game itself, football became more acceptable to the royal family. During the nineties football became an acceptable game, gentle, worthy to represent England as a civilised state. The list of people being recognised by the Queen began to expand and starting in 1994 dozens of players were honoured, including 'Sir' Bobby Charlton, David Beckham 'OBE', Ryan Giggs 'OBE', Bobby Moore 'OBE', Allen Shearer 'OBE' and many others. Football has become part of the British Empire and now that they have learned to eat it with a fork and a knife, as civilised people, they also won a permit to enter to the royal palace.

OBE = Order of the British Empire.

'The deeper the foundations, the stronger the fortress'
(The quote written on the entry sign
to the Emirates Stadium)

A new academy year

The new season in the academies opens. From now on the children will be have a daily routine: the youngsters will arrive the academies in the afternoon, dressed in sweats and equipped with their football boots. The 16-year-old's who have completed their studies within the framework of general education will wake up in their rooms in the morning, wear a tracksuit, pack a bag and arrive at the academy. In the dining room area, they will meet their fellow teammates. They'll chat about the TV series from last night, or the football match they had seen together last weekend. In the first half hour they will eat their breakfast: cereal with milk with seasonal fruits or eggs and cheese. Then they'll sit in the TV corner, chew and blab about the new music video by Madonna, Britney Spears or any other artist on the music channel. Later they will change to the twenty-four hour sports channel to get the latest updates. Afterwards they'll get down to the pitch for their first morning practice, in which they'll work on their technique, speed and teamwork. Right after they will work out in the gym for a couple of hours.

After the first training, they will return to the dining room and pick their lunch from a buffet filled with various pastas, stuffed potatoes and meat. Healthy food to regain the energy they spent in the morning practice, and are about to spend, in case they have an evening practice. In the dining room, they will also meet the young academy players who have just returned from school. Academies are divided into several age groups. The smallest are children up to the age of six, followed by children aged eight, ten and so on until the age of sixteen. In their early years they focus with the lads on basic athletic skills. The kids are working with a ball throughout practices, so that they literally grow up with the ball between their feet, learning to see it as integral part of their bodies. Over the years, they will be taught proper football technique, and when older how to play as part of a team. 16-year-olds and older, who are signed in the academies, are considered 'professionals' in all respects. Their progress is measured in detail by countless professionals, including trainers, fitness instructors, nutritionists, psychologists, educators and personal tutors. Training and matches are filmed on video, edited and uploaded to a website, where the player gets detailed data about his game: speed, passes to losses ratio, performance with and without the ball and so on. Once a week there is a meeting between the player and his personal mentor, which purpose is to conduct personal performance analysis. In the end of the meeting, the two write down points for continuation and for improvement, until next week.

After lunch, the little ones will rest a bit in front of the television or computers, the young will finish their homework, then they will all go to the evening final practice. Each team has two coaches, a fitness trainer, a doctor and a goalkeeper trainer. The goalies train separately and join the team only at the end of the practice. Training sessions are planned to be complex in terms of methodology in order to provide players mental stimulation in addition to the physical one. Practice will not end until everyone fully understands the exercise, and performs it perfectly. After relaxation, they are free to go and rest at home.

Once a week they meet without their tracksuits. They learn proper nutrition, anatomy and physiology, dealing with the media or financial management, in small classes. Foreigners learn English and the local lifestyle. Professional chefs teach the kids healthy cooking, and experts from variety of fields come to provide students with professional classes in case they do not become professional football players. A player, who wishes to be a building contractor if he fails to be a footballer, gets a weekly private lesson with a local contractor. Those who will fulfil the dream will become exemplary English footballers on and off the pitch; they will know what to bring eat, how to behave in front of the camera and what to say in company of strangers. The other will become model British civilians.

On weekends, the teams meet for a friendly match against other academies. Parents come to watch and cheer the young talents. If the weather is clear, the morning becomes a true experience. Families bring coffee, sandwiches and folding chairs, and sit on the sidelines. The academy management encourages them not to interfere with the game. "Good game!" and "Come on lads!" are the common cheering calls. If a player passes inaccurately or misses a ball, you could hear the parents on the sidelines applauded and encourage him to continue the hard work: "bad luck" they say. "Just bad luck! Next time you'll do better!" The game itself is run by referees, who are also children who attend a special school for football referees. The academy doesn't intervene with their judgment, since it's a friendly match, mistakes are forgiven quite quickly.

When the match is over, the young players hurry up to wash and get on the vehicle to take them home to watch the elder's match on TV. Maybe one of the team players will arrive the next day to analyse the match with them. At night, they dream about the day when they will finally play as professionals. Then they will get a shirt with their own number, and fifty thousand supporters will call their names at once. Maybe they will score a goal at the last minute of the match or maybe they'll save a penalty kick. They will be the heroes of the day. All local journalists will know how to spell their name and all four-year-olds will take their finger out of their mouths so they could clap them.

When they have trouble sleeping at night, they worry about the day some foreign talent will take their position in the academy or from the day when they finish their training in the academy and will not find a professional team to play for. It happens. Only a small percentage are signed by a professional team. People still talk about the same marvellous season when Manchester United discovered David Beckham, the Neville brothers, Ryan Giggs and other talents that brought United the Championship. These seasons are rare though. Among those who will not be signed to the Premier League, those who are lucky will play in lower leagues or in other countries. Those who won't make it, will land on soft ground provided by the academy and will become building contractors. Or maybe football trainers.

Academies

Before football clubs in England had 'academies' they had departments for children and youth. Until 1984, these departments were called 'schools of excellence', and they trained children aged nine and above. Although some really great players came out these frameworks, it was not enough to make the English national team the empire it should have be. The national team's failure to win a trophy since the mid-sixties was in the minds of the British sports ministry officials and the Premier League, when in the eighties it was decided to open 'football academies.' Roughly speaking, you can divide the academic development since than to three periods.

Academies that opened in the mid-eighties started to train children as young as six. During that period, each academy worked independently with little supervision by the management of the league. Each club was his own master, and the rules concerning recruiting and training players were not clear. Also, the values of the players was hardly what they are today, so investing in this project was not a priority to the club.

The 1992/93 season was critical for the academies. During this season the Premier League began operating, as we know it today. The new league's management began monitoring the training development of the young children closely. It published a book of rules, which was sent to every coach, parent and player in the academy. It created equal rules between clubs of all academies, and explained the importance of long-term planning. The big money came in from the matches broadcasting agreements with the television networks. It enabled the clubs to allocate funds that were unavailable before to planning and development. Clubs in the professional leagues began cultivating youth academies and colleges. In all of the UK, there were several dozen academies at different professional levels. Investment in young people at that time began to prove itself very quickly. The big winner of investment in 'potentials' at that time was Manchester United, which produced David Beckham, Phil and Gary Neville, Paul Scholes and Ryan Giggs in a single season. Liverpool's academy produced Michael Owen and Steven Gerrard, Chelsea developed John Terry and Ashley Cole was produced by Arsenal. Even the more modest academies boasted of their considerable success. Everton produced Wayne Rooney, Southampton developed Wayne Bridge, Leeds United did well with Paul Robinson and Alan Smith. Little Bournemouth produced Jermain Defoe, and West Ham made it big with Joe Cole, Rio Ferdinand and Frank Lampard, three of the players in the best clubs in the country, and leading national players. Beyond raising the club's pride and increasing the youngsters motivation, which cannot be underestimated, the development of these football players was accompanied by a great deal of money; money which enabled the continued existence of the academy and even helps the management of the first team.

The third period begins in the year 2000 and continues to this day. This is a period that has many advantages, since the professional level in the academies is rising; the country's largest academies, who now understand the potential of young players, invests large amounts of money in trying to make the training conditions of children in the academies with those of the senior team's. Thus, you can find a large swimming pool, gym, kitchen, computer rooms and many staff members in most academies.

This period also has negative characteristics. Building an academy requires long term planning and significant financial resources for the long term. Learning in the academies is free of charge, so these children aren't a source of income in the short term. Academies receive a budget from the British ministry of sports, from the Premier League and from their football club. Income gaps between academies are a direct result of the club's budget, depending on its financial abilities. Also, a large portion of the Premier League club's budget and that of the academies comes from television broadcast agreements. A relegated club loses a most substantial part of its annual budget. That's why, academies of clubs, struggling all year or is likely to struggle during the next five years not to drop to the second league, lose their ability to compete with major academic, whose budgets are secure. As a result, the struggling clubs' academies are restricted from providing the children the same conditions as the successful academies, so that they lose the most talented children. Talented children living in central London, for example, will probably choose to play in Chelsea's academy rather than the one of Fulham, due to the conditions the former offers them, even before mentioning the prestige attached to its name. Football clubs that are turning all their attention in keeping its first team in the league are fighting for their present survival, but with no other choice are giving up on the future.

Chelsea academy

On every weekend, all children aged nine and above play friendly
matches against other academies. The score in these games does not matter.
This is primarily an opportunity to improve the values taught and practiced
in training. In one of the matches that I attended at Chelsea's academy,
there was no referee on the pitch, and the coaches took turns in fulfilling
this role. Charlton's coach was the referee during the first half and Chelsea's
in the second. Each coach is particular strict with his team. This way, when
Charlton's coach is the referee, Chelsea's players get more freedom to
operate on the pitch. Small offences are hardly remarked on, and when an
offence is committed, he declares: "free kick to Chelsea." When it comes to
his team, his judgment is much harsher. Every little touch of an opponent
called a foul, and when a player loses control of the ball near the touchline,
he whistles for a throw in even if the ball did not entirely cross the line.
Players do not resent this; they understand that sticking to the rules, even if
it affects the outcome of this match, will serve them in the future. Chelsea
finishes the first half 4–1 against the visiting team.

In the second half, Chelsea's coach gets the whistle. Like his predecessor,
he is more careful with his team. Charlton's players win in most one-on-one
encounters, and get the ball more often. Nevertheless, it doesn't really help
them; Chelsea's players start the second half with fresh energies, and the
score gap in increasing with blue every attack. Chelsea's coach notices the
power balance and wants his players to change tactics; "play slowly, pass
every ball through the middle of the field, as we did in practice." Chelsea's
game calmed down, Charlton receives more of the ball, and goes out on
attacks. Its coach feels this is where they regained their senses and calls them
to approach: "attitude! Show me the right attitude."

Charlton are playing faster, and score another goal. Chelsea's players do
not get confused, and continue to implement their coach's instructions
carefully. Slow play, every ball goes through the middle of the field. At the
end of the match after the referee's whistle, Chelsea's players mark
themselves a double gain from this match. They won the test result, while
practicing what they learned in training this week in a real match. These
friendly matches provide an opportunity for all to favour the academic

training over the result. To choose the future of their players over the thrill of the moment. Chelsea's academy players took advantage of this opportunity.

Focusing on the training process promises a better outcome at the end of the road. In an interview I was conducting with Mr Smith, director of Arsenal's academy, he elaborates: "Our goal is to train players to be able to play for us when they grow up, and generate players we can sell to other clubs in order to finance the continued operation of the academy in the future."

"The state invests a lot of money in the academies for the sake of raising a future generation to the English national team," I point out. "Does this have any influence on the goals you, as an academy, set for yourselves?"

"It does not bother me. I'm the director of Arsenal's academy; therefore, the only thing standing before me is the success of our football club. Indirectly, the success of the academies have an impact on the level of the Premier League, on the success of the English clubs in European Cup games and on the quality of the players of the English national team. Yet this is an indirect consequence, not a goal in itself."

"What about academic success in recent years?" I ask. "Can you identify any players that were trained in the academy and became professionals?"

"In recent years we have good outcomes. The academy brought out the goalkeeper Stuart Taylor, David Bentley, who was even invited to join the national team, and Steve Sidwell, who played for Chelsea and Aston Villa. In addition, we sold three players to football clubs of lower leagues. But it's still too early to test the result. Training of young people today you will come to fruition only in the future," he concludes.

Scott Sinclair and Ben Sahar emerged from Chelsea's Academy. Sinclair is the academy's great pride because he is the first player that grew in the academy after its reorganisation. Up to the half of the 2007/08 season, he became a regular first team player. Sinclair was loaned to few clubs from the Premier League, in 2015 has signed for Aston villa. Up until 2015 Chelsea sent no less than 31 football players on loan. This is unprecedented! Celebrated clubs like Manchester United and Liverpool are also producing younger players at the academies and those are beginning to win the trust of the first team's managers. In recent years, West Ham's academy produced

Michael Carrick who was sold to Tottenham and then to Manchester United, and Southampton's academy produced Theo Walcott, who plays for Arsenal. However, it seems that relative to previous years, academies find it difficult to produce first team players whereas major academies take over this market. It changes the young English footballer's movement direction. Chelsea's academy set a goal to send one player to the first team and loan five players to lower league clubs each year, starting in 2010. This is an ambitious target, but even if they can achieve it only partially, it will change the map completely. So, instead of small club players being signed by the major clubs, as was common until the new millennium, now more players are trained by the major clubs and sign with the small ones. It is a magic cycle: the massive financial investment creates an advantage in favour of the rich clubs already in the children's training stage. This benefit will increase as they grow up, and the players would be higher priced. The rich clubs will stay rich and the poor ones will go on fighting for their survival.

Scouting

The scouting system in the academy changes according to its financial ability. Small academies hire about five scouts; Medium ones hire about ten; the large ones have a lot more. Chelsea's academy, for example, has over thirty scouts in the UK and abroad, who are responsible of scouting players at the age of six to sixteen from South London, and a couple of more brilliant players from around the world. Overall, each academy in the UK has one hundred and eighty to two hundred children training at any given time. The children receive new sets of kit, boots and other accessories on request. From the age of sixteen, players get to receive a weekly scholarship; the management of the Premier League determines the amount annually. These settings promise that young football talents from England and the world will be discovered, and will be able to play in the academy almost regardless of their family's financial state.

All matches, except for the Reserve League, are played as friendly matches, and not on competitive terms.

"Only amateur leagues now play competitive football. All professional leagues in England, like us, play friendly games," says director of the Chelsea academy. The rationale is clear: wherever the importance of the final result is low, emphasis is placed on the individual's improvement, so there is much more space for training and improvement. There is collaboration between the academies and the referees' academies, so that young boys who want to be football referees when they grow up, come to run the matches. Because the result is not recorded, their training conditions improve. They are not required to impress anyone, and mistakes are accepted with understanding as part of the process.

Many times you can hear parents on the sidelines asking: "What's the score on that pitch?" or, "how are the boys doing in other pitches?" At the beginning of my research I also used this sentence as an excuse to start a conversation with the parents. It served me, with limited success, until one of the mothers answered: "I don't know what the score is, tell you the truth, I don't really care. My son plays as a striker, and I just want him to finish this match safe and sound." After hearing this answer, I moved to other, safer opening sentences. "Nice weather today, isn't it?" classic, always works.

Learning, is then, the main issue in the academies. Future outcome are considered, but there is no pressure on children to provide the results during their training period. In my interview with Mr Smith I asked him when it was likely that we will see results of all the work invested in the academy in the first team.

"Patience," he replied. "We are working in this format for only eight years. When we began training the children they were only six. It would take another four years before we can see the results. It's still too early to judge us at the moment, give us a chance." That sentence reminded me of the white letter caption written on a red background that greets the players at the Emirates Stadium: 'The deeper the foundations, the stronger the fortress'. Academies take this sentence very seriously.

Some tactics and moving on

Changing attitudes to training

Before coming to England I did not know much about the professional aspects of English football. I knew the some about hooligans supporters, recognised few of the players' names, and was sad in memorial days honouring the people who died under tragic circumstances in the past. The bottom line is I had no idea what the meaning of 'English football' is, and what makes it different from Italian football, let's say. So… before I packed my bags for the trip, I consulted a few insiders.

"English football is very physical, it is characterised in long balls, speed and many opportunities near the goal", they said. Already in my first visit in the academies, I could definitely see how accurate were the last two descriptions: all training and friendly matches were played at such speed that made me a little worried about the young children's respiratory systems. Goal opportunities were matters of routine that no one took to heart unless it ended with an impressive group performance or a ball in the net. However, regarding the first two narratives – the physical and playing long balls – I wasn't sure.

My favourite games in the academies were played by children 'under 10 years old' (U10). The children in this age group played against rival groups the first time, and during a tournament of two matches played in parallel, each on a half-size pitch and in teams of six against six. Because they are in the preliminary stage, coaches and referees are very attentive, and this trilateral relationship between the players, coaches and the referee, is fascinating. All the matches I've seen at academies it was difficult to notice any touch, not to mention physical struggle. Attempts to keep the ball, control it or win it were made with minimum physical contact, minimum body interference and maximum concentration on the ball. At first I thought it was so because these are children; After all, at a young age the body is still developing, and any harm to it can be irreversible. Therefore, great caution is necessary. However, it was the same at the matches of the older children on age groups U12, U14 and U16 physical tackles were rare.

Actually, except for one incident (out of dozens of matches), when two opposing players came down too strong on the ball, I do not recall any incident in which physical incidences were a factor to consider during match-ups of the academies games.

The answer can probably be found in the changes that English football went through in the last fifty years. In 2007, BBC television network produced a documentary called A Game of Two Eras: 1957 v 2007 which examines the transformation of English football throughout the last fifty years by comparing the FA Cup Finals in 1957 to that in 2007. For this purpose the programme makers interviewed writers, journalists and football players who took part in the 1957 Cup Final between Aston Villa and Manchester United. They also interviewed an analyst who's currently employed by FIFA and UEFA. The conclusion that came up from the film was clear; although in the earlier matches there were less fouls and fewer cards, English football in the fifties was, without a doubt, a much more physical and a much tougher game. Deliberate tackles weren't unusual, and were even encouraged by the coach and the crowd at the stands. Even tackling from behind, now prohibited by the rules, were acceptable. The common practice of the game at that time was: fast, physical and simple; it was reflected in passes of long balls forward in every opportunity. Complex formations were not as common as they are now and as can be seen by the percentage of completed passes. In the 1957 Cup Final, Manchester United took the lead in this parameter with sixty-nine percent success in completing a pass versus sixty-three percent to Aston Villa. Fifty years later, Manchester United had eighty-two percent pass completion; and Chelsea, the same final rival with eighty-three.

The transition to a tactical game from a physical game was the result of a change in the philosophy of the game, with the opening of English football to Europe and the world. It manifests itself most clearly by the change in training methods in all groups; In the fifties, most training was dedicated to improving and preserving the physical strength using exercises brought from the British Army, which were comprised mainly of long-distance running and stair training. The emphasis on technique and tactics was scarce, and most of the training was carried out without a ball at all. Training looks different today. At the same time while improving the physical fitness of the players, tactical training is an indispensable matter. In addition, the importance of ball control has risen over the years, and today one can see children as young as four with a ball which is a quarter size of their body, trying to run with the ball across the pitch, while passing through the cones.

The emphasis on a thoughful game and its preference over the physical, traditional English game are a dramatic change made by the coaches in academies in recent years. In addition, the careers of football players would be extended following the academy matches training. An English player who began training at the young age of six may play until he's about the age of thirty-four, facing nearly thirty years of severe physical challenges, at least once a week. Tactical game can reduce the risk of injuries and the accelerated erosion of the body.

Generally speaking, you can divide the process of footballers training in the academies to three stages. First is for children aged six to nine. This phase of training focuses mainly in developing coordination and working with the ball. Physically speaking, this developmental stage is most appropriate for improving coordination. Children this age can go through each of the positions and do not professionalise in any one in particular. The exercises are designed so that in each performance, the kids move through several positions one by one, while switching between positions is very fast. For example, a child goes from a corner flag and needs to move the ball all the way to a diagonal position while avoiding other players on the way. When he succeeds, he moves to play in a defensive position and tries to prevent another player from doing the same exercise. In the next stage the coach adds another element, a kick for example; so that in one drill each child gets to practice his kicks, his movement with the ball and playing in a defence position.

The trainings of children aged six to nine is usually the most entertaining and happy. The coaches, who require special talent to train kids that age, are trying to walk between the raindrops; on the one hand to give a children the opportunity to improve their skills. On the other hand – and this is perhaps even more important – they try to keep the children's joy for life and love for the game. Thus, instruction is not given to them as a command, but a request. In case a ball deviates, which happens often because of over-enthusiasm, coaches don't stop the exercise or raise their voices. "Adam, go get the ball, please," he's asked. And there he goes to get it. To give positive reinforcement trainers in many cases stop the practice to applaud and compliment. The coaches sometimes join the kids for several exercises, thus increasing their sense of harmony in the team.

With the children's process of mental and physical maturation, the trainers of the academy begin to work with the children on their technique and tactics. At this stage, the training becomes more complex, when the children are required the ability to think and analyse actions during and after the match. During practice, it is common to hear the coaches translate the kids' physical effort into mental thinking. Shooting the ball is not only an action done by the foot, rather an action done with your head: "concentrate! Work with your heads," they tell them. "Spend some time to think!" Even when they stretch, the young coach encourages them to think by asking the players to choose their own exercises. While doing so, he asks them which muscles are stretched in any given exercise, briefly reminding them some of the frontal physiology classes they learned in the academy. The coach prepares the practice while trying to maximise the development all of the children's necessary skills.

At the age of sixteen, the students own coordination skills, technical abilities and are trained to analytically analyse the game. At the same time they also complete their mandatory schooling in generic schools, so they are considered to be football players in all manners. They receive a salary from the club and are signed on an obligating contract. The nature of work becomes more individual, as each player is appointed with a personal mentor who follows his development at all levels. After every practice or match, the player fills out a progression report in which he lists how many minutes he played, in what position, in what point he felt comfortable on the pitch, and which he need to be focus in his next trainings. The workouts are divided at this point to two parts: morning and evening training. Morning training is group training for all age groups. In this training, the players specialise in their positions in a group setting. On the afternoon training, the children divide into groups according to their skills that require improvement. Those who need to increase muscle mass will spend the workout in the gym, those who require speed will be spending the afternoon doing agility exercises on the pitch, and those who need to work with the ball will find themselves in another corner of the pitch, kicking or heading the ball towards the coach. There is high level of supervision during practice, yet they always keep in mind the player enjoyment throughout the practice.

From the age of sixteen players are divided into two groups: 'U18' and the reserve team. The first one still plays friendly matches where results are not recorded; the second plays in a league. Matches are mostly filmed and uploaded to each of the player's personal website. After the match, he will watch the video, and together with the coach and personal mentor they will analyse his performance on the pitch.

Occasionally, one of these players will be invited to practice with the first team. Beyond the experience the young player acquires during his training with a professional team, his performance is tested using advanced devices throughout the practice. His running speed and distance are being measured, as well as the strength of his kick and even the chemical composition of his sweat, which testifies on the extent of his effort during training. Also, training with the first team has another function; the boy gets to know the team in which he will, hopefully, play with when he grows up while allowing the team manager to guide him.

Most chances are that when a student finishes his training in the academy at the age of eighteen, he will not immediately begin to play with the first team. One of the most important changes made in academies in recent years is expanding the definition of 'child', hence extending the ideal training period in the academy until the age of twenty-one. The rationale behind this change is the understanding that the young players who complete the academies successfully at the age of eighteen and sign with the top teams in the league are likely to spend their first few seasons sitting on the bench. Loosing so many match hours compared to the amount they were used to in the academy, can harm their mental and physical fitness. That's why they seek to continue developing the players for three more years. The favoured option for players between the ages of eighteen and twenty-one is a loan to a club from a lower league, while the academy coaches continue to monitor their progression. After they will get all physical, mental and psychological tools they can and gain experience the more chance they will have more success in the transition from the warm, protective nest into their first competitive league.

To summarise, the player who began training at the academy at the age of six will stay there for fifteen years! There are only a few professions in the world in which the training period is longer than that of an English footballer.

Intelligent thinking

In addition to the changes to the training programme on the pitch in recent years, the academies increase the amount of hours dedicated to learning in frontal classes as well. In one of the classes I attended, the coach divided the children into three groups, according to their positions on the pitch – defence, midfield and attack. White pages with expressions of character written on them are scattered on about a dozen tables across the room. The children are asked to find the features that a player in their position needs to have. Throughout their entire work the coach calls to them "work as a team." This is how they develop two acute features for the sake of their future: analytic ability and teamwork. After twenty minutes of bewilderment the players go back to sitting with the groups they worked with. The coach gathers their answers. "What are the essential features of a goalkeeper?" He turns his question to the defence group and writes their answers on the board. "Ability to communicate with other players on the pitch, concentration, alertness, decisions making". He goes on: "Which features do goalkeepers and defenders need? Speed, Communication, leadership, passing skills, superiority in one on one struggles, and ability to cover large areas. Wingers need speed, ability to run with the ball, control, passing skills and the ability to assist and score goals. Offensive players need vigilance, wisdom, kicking strength in both legs, speed, high work rate and good control in the air".

To generate interest among students the coach connects between theory and practice. Which of these features makes Drogba a good striker? The board fills up quickly, students enthusiastically collaborate, and coach compliments them for the hard work they did. After ninety minutes of theoretical lesson they go to the pitch and play some ball. In the next couple of training sessions the coach will remind them of things they learned in this lesson. "Do you remember what are the features required of a winger? Which of these features would you say you lacked in the last practice?" The knowledge and understanding acquired during frontal classes will be implemented during trainings; so will the sense of hard work, teamwork and the coaches' comments.

The differences, if so, between traditional English football and that learned in the academies today are reflected in changing the characteristics of the game; the game is now less physical, more tactical. It's still fast yet more patient and effective, with calculated passes and preference of midfield instead of quick passes from defence to offence. Playing with the head is preferred over acting spontaneously. Physical persistence is less rewarded than 'smart', alternative solutions such as group collaboration, identifying an available player, double and triple passes and creating space. The training sessions are planned in ascending level of complexity, where in the concluding exercises children are expected to employ all their senses, to be able to analyse situations and react quickly on the pitch.

The academy gives science and rational thought a significant place in their training. Coaches and educators of English football are able to associate scientific knowledge into football, which has been traditionally considered a game of the masses. They do a good job; today, 'smart' or 'intelligent' are two of the more common compliments a football player can receive; and smart players create smart games, too. Defining the game as intelligent also entails economic as well as political and image related profits. Club owners earn from selling tickets for the first team matches at high prices, players and coaches justify the astronomic salaries they receive, and together they manage to convince us that the modern game is much more interesting than when it belonged to the working class.

After football turned from a physical, spontaneous game to a clever, tactical game, and the students learned to collaborate as a team and specialise in many positions on the pitch, they lacked only one trait to turn them into being real English football players. This is perhaps the most critical trait of them all: the children have to be good lads.

Good lads play football

Good young lads

Ten teams wearing white-red (Arsenal's home kit) and yellow-brown (away kit) are now playing on five of the pitches at Arsenal's academy. This is an internal tournament where youth academy players of all ages play against themselves. Three pitches are designated for the older boys, playing eleven against eleven. The kiddos, swimming in their extra-small kits, play on half-pitch six against six. The proud parents standing on the lines encourage their children, and on the way they also cheer the children playing in the opposing team; After all, here at the academy, everyone knows everyone.

I sit on the touchline of the young children's pitch. The London summer sun is touching on everyone, encouraging us to wear shirts and sandals, while children are asked to drink plenty of waters so they won't dehydrate. The referee is a young boy, maybe fifteen years old, dressed in an official black kit with a whistle in his mouth. On his first throw-in call he tells one of the players to stand behind the white line and throw the ball in; the boy tries, but in the heat of the match, he steps on the line. The referee stops the match, asks for the ball and repeats the instructions. "You must stand with both feet behind the line," he explains patiently. But the mistake is repeated; in the heat of the moment the toddler steps on the line again while throwing the ball into the pitch. The referee, incredibly patient, stops the match again, ask for the ball again, and again, asks to repeat the action. "When you grow up," he explains, "you will lose this ball if you step on the line. You must stand with both feet behind it." All other coaches and parents are watching them without blinking; they understand how important it is that children absorb the rules so early in their childhood, even if it comes at the expense of continuity of the match. When the young player finally handles the ball right, he wins cheers from all sides, including the referee who flatters him, "great ball, great ball!"

The game is divided into thirds, thirty minutes each. Each team scores a large number of goals. The nets are large, the goalkeepers are small, and so it is not surprising. When one of team scores, cheers are heard from all sides. Immediately afterwards, all parents take time to encourage the other team. "Bad luck, bad luck," they tell the players. In Academy matches, they are not punished for mistakes.

The calls ranges from "good game" to those who succeed in moving and scoring the ball, to "bad luck" to those who make mistakes. At some point during the match, parents start using abbreviations. Instead of calling "bad luck", they just call "luck" and "lucky". Whoever comes in at the middle of the match, doesn't necessarily understands why specifically those who missed receive a positive calls such as "luck". The kids themselves do not celebrate their goals with hugging and jumping. They just raise a thumbs-up to the players who were involved in the attack that led to the goal, or pat on the shoulder of the goalkeeper who conceded the goal, to encourage him.

The first third of the game ends 3–3. The children sit alongside the coach, drinking water and listen to what they need to improve in their play. When they go on to play in the second third, the referee disappears, but no one seems to feel his absence. The referee disappearance is part of the work system. From now on, the children themselves will take care of to the fair play and protection of the rules. And they do so; throw-ins are now made when both feet of player are, without a doubt, behind the white line. Also, when players falls while fighting for the ball, no one is looking for the referee to whistle for an offence; no one, except for one parent, who later receives embarrassed looks from parents standing beside him.

During this third I meet one of the academic coaches, who watches the young children's play, like me. His name is Ernie, and his about to go to a pitch downtown to watch a nine-year-old boy, who's been said to be skilful. Before he leaves the academy, he takes his time to tell me about the training programme of the early ages.

"What do you teach the kids?" I ask him.

"We are mainly letting them play with the ball, but forget about the game for now. The most important thing we want to teach them at this stage is to be good young lads," he says.

"Who are 'good young lads'?" I question.

"Good young lads!" He repeats the same words, as if repeating it again will make the description clearer. "Young lads are good kids who know how to give respect. We try to teach them to respect the ball and the game they are playing. Respect the kits they wear. Therefore, it is rare, for example, that at the end of a day's training, all the equipment that left the storeroom in the morning won't be returned. The children learn to respect the equipment, respect the game and respect themselves. I always tell them, 'The ball is like your friend, you must know how to respect it, so that it will respect you back'."

In the foolishness of the moment I tell him that where I come from, they use to tell the soldiers the same sentence about their weapons. Ernie looks at me with a sad look, which make me decide to leave my Israeli anecdotes for Israelis only.

Ernie continues: "The kids must respect their trainer and the referee. They have to respect their parents, the kids they play with and against and respect themselves. You know, they just have to be young nice lads", he summarises with few short word what is, in my eyes, the new English football ideology. Respect.

We had not noticed the second third of the game is already over, and we're in the late third. Ernie had to go check out the new prodigy boy, and I stayed to watch the final moments of the match. The parents say that the result now is 6–5 in favour of the team wearing the official club's home kit. The referee is again on the pitch, and when he whistles to the end of the game, all players come up to shake his hand as well as the hands of the players they just played against, although they train together every day. After the handshakes, each team sits around their coach for a short summary talk. Meanwhile, they take off their boots and shin pads. The parents are waiting for their offspring on the touchline. When the talk ends the kids get up, stand on the parallel touchline away from their parents and start running toward them.

"In line, in line," the coach calls them, and they get in one line and start the releasing run over again. The parents standing on the other side applaud all the players; thank them for their effort. The players enjoy the attention; clap back, while keeping the white line, which separates them from their parents, just as if it was a line in a real football stadium, which separates the pitch from the stands.

Play by the rules

One weekend later, this time I'm at Chelsea's academy in a match with the kids from Tottenham's academy. In one of the moves, Chelsea's kid's attack, a series of mistakes by Tottenham's defensive players leaves three blue players in front of one white player. The ball is shot towards the net, but only hits the post. A rebound is kicked weakly and passes the goal line. Tottenham's goalkeeper is confused, and kicks it out too late. According to the rules of the game, this is a perfectly legal goal! However, the referee doesn't approve it, because the goal was a result of a series of mistakes made by the visiting team rather than the good teamwork of Chelsea's players. The players do not resent the decision and continue playing. Later they make some good moves, and receive a standing ovation from viewing parents. The applause they get is as a result of their good performances, rather than the goals they score. When a blue Chelsea player scores an easy goal from a rather comfortable location, he wins relatively less clapping compared to the applause a defensive player gets when he gets himself out of the tight pressure of a rival players, runs forward with the ball and kicks powerfully towards the net. Although the ball only hits the bar and flies out. This performance wins enthusiastic cheers from all spectators, visitors and hosts. Generally, this environment encourages developing abilities; the result is temporary. Overall, the result is a marginal issue in these matches. Although in some cases you can hear parents catching up on the outcome of the game or another, that question is only an excuse for deep analysis of the match, particularly the performance of the players who participated.

As in Arsenal, here as well, much attention is paid to playing the game by the rules. When Chelsea's goalkeeper kicks the ball forward to his team, and kicks it outside, the match stops and the goalie is asked to repeat the kick once again. He manages to do it right on the second attempt, and almost never repeats the same mistake again. Beyond that, they keep a high strictness as regards to fouls; almost each contact between two players is called as a foul. All these features highlight the ideals of 'fair play' in England. English football is shaped by these values from the early stage of the academic training.

Behaviour code

England's football academies teach children what is the ideal image of an English footballer to which they should aspire. The behaviour code signed by the children at the start of each season states that the student should: "Look smart, play smart. Shirt inside shorts, socks up, boots are clean."

The behaviour code specifies that the children are supposed to shake hands firmly at the end of each game. On the pitch, they learn to respect the ball, the kits, themselves, their friends, their opponents and the referees. They learn not to be too pleased with their successes, as well as not to collapse from disappointments. These features shape the way they will come to perceive the game of football in the future. Moreover, it reflects the way they will perceive themselves, their colleagues, their opponents and authority figures, and overall reflects their general behaviour in the English society when they grow up. Even off the pitch they behave politely. Although there is no behaviour code that requires it, when they come close to the parents lounge, they walk on their tiptoes so that their noise boots don't disturb the peace.

The models of behaviour designed for children of the academies can be imagined as a pyramid. The first stages of training highlights three key features necessary for each player: a healthy lifestyle, proper psychological development and good medical condition. Healthy lifestyle includes the food the children eat, their behaviour with friends on and off the pitch, at home and at school, and the way they spend their leisure time. Academies advise them to divide their leisure time between studying and promoting other interests except for football. Maintaining physical fitness will promote them on the pitch, but more importantly, will prevent them from binding to negative elements in society. Drugs, alcohol and criminal activity are not mentioned here, because these are inviolable taboos. So is cigarette smoking. Their psychological development is examined by professionals and measured by two key parameters: high energy and the right attitude. These qualities are the foundations. The player skills on the pitch come only at the higher stages in the pyramid.

Assuming the kids of the academy have the features that appear in the imaginary pyramid base, you can go on to the next level. At this point there are two essential features; high physical ability on the pitch, technique and tactics. The children's physical ability is indeed closely monitored by doctors at the academy, but the children themselves have an important role in watching their personal health, whether as part of an ongoing preventive treatment, including proper eating habits and training discipline outside the academy, or in informing the coach on all potential illness or injury. Academy players would like, of course, to take part in every game, but they are asked to take responsibility and to be honest, and sit on the bench if they feel that they are not at their best and that participation can harm them in the long term. The fact is that all matches are non-competitive friendly matches, sending them the message that their physical health is more important than participation in a single match. Finally, at the top of the pyramid are the child's professional skills on the pitch. These skills are a direct result of the acquiring all of the features in the pyramid base.

Young footballers therefore need some essential features without which they cannot be accepted as full-fledged players in the academy, and unlikely to succeed as professional English footballers in the future. Apart from their ability on the football pitch, they should show respect to themselves, their team and to authority figures. They should learn teamwork and demonstrate positive energy. They should know how to put together their own healthy diet and how to develop other interests outside of football. This long and holistic training process will have an impact on the way they play the game in the next ten to twenty years. It will also affect the way English football will look like in the coming decades.

Role model

But what happens when the role model that the children are encouraged to look up to, does not exactly corresponds to the ideal characteristics defining the 'English football player?' When going into the Arsenal's academy parent's lounge, you'll notice some pictures of players who studied in the academy. The most famous image is that of Ashley Coles. Cole was educated at the Arsenal academy, but eventually signed a contract with Chelsea, a team so hated by Arsenal supporters. During matches between the two teams, whenever Cole touches the ball, a thunderous 'boo' is heard from the section of Arsenal supporters. However, this is not the only problem. Ashley Cole is also featured quite a bit in newspaper gossip columns in not very positive contexts such as casual sex with women. Cole was married to a pop star, and their romantic relationship were reported in great detail in cheap gossip magazines.

Even on the pitch Ashley Cole is not a player without problems. In one of Chelsea's Premier League matches, the referee decided to give Cole a yellow card following a foul he committed against an opponent. Cole refuses to accept the referee's decision, and turned his back demonstratively. This act by Cole is condemned on every platform. The exact quotes from the conflict between Cole and the referee are published all over the media. Everyone's trying to figure out what happened there, maybe find a reasonable explanation to Cole's behaviour, but with no great success. There is no explanation for such behaviour; this is not the way an English player is expected to behave.

I ask the director of Arsenal's academy what kind of role model Cole is for the children? Without hesitation, Mr Smith answers me confidently: "Cole is an international professional football player and a player in England's national team. We are very proud of him." Before finishing his sentence, he was already shifting uncomfortably in his chair. Before I say another word, he says: "Look, I know what you think. We are also uncomfortable with his behaviour and his personal life. Today we can't do anything about it, but we try to apply the lessons we have learned from Cole training every day here in the academy.

Good family

David's move

One Friday evening I was again invited to have dinner at Johnny's house. Roy, the youngest son in the family, and David, his friend from Arsenal's academy, are also present, although they have sad faces. They tell us that a collective decision made by the academy's management and professional staff, determined that David will be loaned to a Third Division club in the north of England, a five-hour drive from London and from Roy. While David tells us the story his back is straight, his neck is long, only his eyes look down from time to time. His maturity is impressive. There are detailed explanations why it is best for a young player to first sign with a lower league club before signing with a club from the Premier League, I remember the things the managers of the academy told me in the past; he will get more playing time, get used to playing in front of a crowd and learn to cope under pressure. But no rational explanation, I feel, will help dampen the sense of disappointment around the table.

Johnny and Roy's mother serves an appetiser of stuffed vine leaves, and guests fill their plates mainly because they are uncomfortable doing otherwise. The feeling of disappointment dulls our appetite.

"The life of a footballer is not easy," says the mother as she serves bowls of rice and meat to the table. "But you, don't give up. Play hard and you'll finally succeed, I'm sure."

"And how much will they pay you there?" The pragmatic father wants to know. His appetite, on the other hand, was not ruined and he checks his plate to see he has just enough of every dish served on the table.

David tries at first to keep the details of the agreement to himself, but in light of their insistence he reveals the numbers. His salary, which is not higher than that of other footballers, but nevertheless impressive compared to the average income of the family. The father gives a long whistle. "Well then, maybe life is not so difficult, is it?" He concludes in his mouth full. David smiles awkwardly. Johnny joins his dad and calculates how many shifts will have to work at the coffee shop to earn a similar amount. When he finally concludes, he gets angry and discouraged. "I could have made a great movie with a budget like this," he says. Only Roy, who's confidence and fluency of speech usually liven up the dinners, is silent.

The Mother asks David how is he planning to move all his equipment from his house in London up to the north. He tells her that his family members were coming to England soon and help with the transfer.

"Will Arsenal help?" the father is interested.

"The club will take care of the technical transfer, my family will help making the apartment a home. They will stay with me for few weeks and then I'll have to take care of myself. I know how to cook a little, and I will learn how to do laundry too."

"He's a big boy," John added. "When I was his age, I moved to live alone."

"Moving from north London to a flat in the city centre is not quite as difficult as moving to a different country, a new city and a different language," I bet. Johnny's father mumbles some undetectable words. David smiles at me in a silent foreigners' understanding and only Roy is silent.

Three hours later, when the parents go up to bed, we sit and drink a glass of Brandy before our last farewell. Johnny, who did not quite know how to drink, almost fell asleep after having one drink. David is mostly silent. Both of our glasses are the only ones who remained exactly as they were when he poured the bitter liquid into it. David is forbidden to drink, and in general, he is exhausted from a long evening of conversation in a second language, and now seeks only to rest. Roy looked deep in thoughts most of the time. He finished one drink, and already pours the second. Under the brandy's influence, he tells David what he couldn't say in front of everyone. "You know, friend, your living hurts me like when the doctor told me that my career was finished. I heard the words, but just the look in his eyes made me realise how final the decision is. To this day I can't remember a word he said, only the look in his eyes. And I heard you talking all night, but I don't remember a word. Only from your gaze I know how sad you are. I'm sad too. I don't want you to go." And a moment before he sinks in silence he adds: "and I want to go with you so bad!'

Football parents

It is not easy being a family of a young football player. They need to make sure he gets to practices and matches, to take care that he eats right and ensure that he follows the instructions of the academy. Parents and families have an important part in the training process of the child, so the academy players come mostly from families with at least moderate social-economic status, families that have the ability to invest time and energy in raising and nurturing the child.

An away game of Chelsea's academy brings me to the Watford academy, where I meet a kind grandfather who came with his grandson for a friendly match. He tells me: "My daughter and her husband are the parents of three children. The big one plays in the academy. He supposed to come here five times a week immediately after school training, and once at the weekend for a match. No buses run from their house to the academy so they have to bring him themselves. The problem is that they both work until five PM every day. They have two more children. The first loves music, he plays the trumpet and the little one is fond of aviation and participates in an aero-modelling afternoon class. It's a great difficulty for two working parents to mobilise each child to his afternoon activities. I try to help."

Premier League limiting rules required a change in the geographic location of the training complexes. A British law that determines how the academy should look also indicates the technical specification of the academy. For example, a club that wishes their youth department to attain the status of 'academy', should have at least six grass pitches (for 10 or more teams), one artificial surface pitch, one indoor playing area measuring 60 yards by 40 yards, changing rooms equal in number to the number of teams (including visiting teams), adequate study area for 40 students, parents' lounge and more. These physical constraints forced the clubs in London to give up the expensive training complexes in the city, and move to the suburbs. Chelsea's academy is located in a small town south of London. To get there from the central London, Chelsea/Fulham area, you have to leave home at least two hours in advance, to get to Waterloo station and from there take the intercity train to the south. Thus, taking the children from school to the academy became more complex. 'When I trained in Arsenal's youth section," Ted, who is a former Arsenal player who is now about forty and works at the Club's Community Department, tells me, "directors of the Youth Department would give us money for buses, and we would make this route, every day the same way, on our own. Today, due to the change in the geographical location of the facilities, parents are an integral part of the child's training."

Beyond the time they are asked to invest, academies require parents to adapt certain code of conduct so that they will serve as a positive role model for their children. At the beginning of each season the parents sign a binding document that defines how to behave at any given time at the academy and at home. The code of conduct requires them to praise good work, refrain from criticising lapses, and set a good example to the students. Special classes designed for parents only, during which they learn what is expected of them as parents and educators. A football player will fail to match the model that the academic management is trying to produce, if he doesn't have the proper support and behaviour model to aspire to. Bernard, the Arsenal academy coach, tell me about the connections between the socio-economic status of parents and their children's success in football academies.

"Listen to this story: About a year ago I encountered a boy of ten, a natural player. Every time he touched ball, he did wonders for his team. His name is Keith. It was impossible to beat him in a one-on-one, and his footwork could make some of the players in the world's best leagues jealous. I immediately brought him to try out for Arsenal, of course. He impressed all of the professional staff. He played with players in his age level, and did not fall from them for a moment, it was as if had played here since birth, even without him ever participating in a professional practice before. We decided that we had to sign him. As we do in such cases, we immediately invited his parents and prepared the forms.

The parents did not arrive for the meeting. His father – who we later discovered to be a single parent of three children, said that if we want his son, we would have to come to their house. In an unusual step we got there. We were eager for the small talent to sign with us. When we finally met, we discovered that there are still some obstacles on the way. First, the father insisted that his older son, who was fourteen, also signs with the academy. We tested him. He was, to say the least, not as good as his younger brother, but we were prepared to accept him if only his brother will sign. It was not the only problem. The father, who had to work two jobs due to their difficult economic situation, demanded that we take upon ourselves the responsibility of taking their children to the academy and back to all practices and matches. In addition, if there were not enough problems so far, it turned out that in his school Keith is quite a 'trouble-maker' who does not invest in his studies and makes troubles for his teachers. After consultation at the offices of the academy, we decided to forgo the signing of the two brothers. They might have been suitable to another club, but for us, they were just not good enough".

As mentioned, the location of the training facility produced a phenomenon of 'football moms and dads', parents that drive their children to the academy every afternoon and weekends, stay with them during training and games, and then return them home. Football parents are able to work only half jobs, if any. Parents who can afford this pleasure apparently do not drink their cup of tea at the same place where Keith's dad drank his pint of beer.

Socio-economic status is significant even when it comes to the child's behaviour in school. The obedient players that the academy administrators want the children to be, usually grow in very certain neighbourhoods in the city. The reluctance felt by the Arsenal academy to signing a child who is considered 'trouble', is not accidental. Football academies avoid signing 'problematic' children, either at home or at school, as their conduct consumes energy from the system, no matter how talented they may be. Thus, it is likely that some of the senior players in English football, who grew up in the sixties and left school before the end of their mandatory education to make a living, would not have received a contract in the academy today.

Go back to our story. Bernard continues: "We've got a very tough fight for young children who play good football. The most dramatic struggle is between Chelsea and Arsenal; Chelsea have financial capabilities much higher than ours, and are trying, through their money, to compete with our academic success. In the end, Chelsea's scouts spotted Keith, met with the father, and agreed to all his terms. The older boy joined to the U14 team, and special taxis were sent every day to pick up the two brothers from home and take them back. During the first year the older brother retired from the academy, thought the small one continues to play there to this day. We still can't tell if he will be a great player one day, we will have to wait eight years to find that out."

"In retrospect, if you knew about his future signing with Chelsea, would you do things differently to sign Keith?" I dare to ask.

"No, but I hope Keith and his father would have planned their life differently, so they could have signed with us."

One sunny day

Marcus and Twinny

Just before the winter comes, we get to indulge in some rare days of pleasant sunshine. Our clothes are still warm, the wind is cool but gentle, and it's sunny in the Arsenal academy. Greetings begin with mutual delight about the weather: "a wonderful day today, isn't it?" Indeed wonderful, if you know what I mean?" You can tell the people in England agree according to the number of question marks they place in the end of each sentence; usually locals prefer to formulate as questions only facts they are confident about completely. When they want to introduce a fact that they are not sure about it, they formulate it in the form of a personal opinion. For example "For me Arsenal would be in first place at the end of the season. They play great, don't they?" Well, while regarding the quality of their play there is no one who will argue, whether they'll finish the season as champions, the opinions vary.

The mood at the Arsenal academy, in any occasion, is great. The first team are playing well and lead the league, and academy matches have precedence over club rivals. I walk across the five pitches in which friendly matches against Millwall are currently taking place. I stop to witness the two U10 teams. In the first half six Arsenal players play against six Millwall players, and in the second half the teams switch. The result of the match is a summary of the goals in both matches, but it is not really important. Most parents and other supporters are mainly engaged in performance. I recognise Marcus in the first team and Twinny in the second. I know Marcus mainly from the year photos hanging on the walls of the academy. This is the first time that I get to see him play. Marcus is a skinny boy, short, not well built. In team photos he always sits in the front row, so that the camera could catch him. He plays up front wearing shirt number five. His facial tone is a light mocha colour, his features are sensitive, his hair is frizzy and messy, the kind that never surrenders to a comb or a hairbrush. Compared to the rest of the children he looks fragile and weak. I wonder if he has the skills to cope with the Millwall players, who are at least a head taller than him. While he's sitting on the grass next to the coaches, he is relaxed and calm. He occasionally claps after an impressive performance, but he doesn't try to attract the attention of the coach hoping he will let him on too. He doesn't notice the parents nor all the kickup around.

In the second half he goes up to play. First he moves without the ball, up and down, depending on the pace of his team, which controls the pitch. After a few minutes he gets the ball when he's in the centre of the field. I'm excited. Marcus makes me feel sympathetic. He seemed a little bit distracted, with eyes that reveal nothing. A bit of an outsider. Marcus begins to run with the ball. His marker is taller than him, and Marcus had to run a larger number of steps to get around him. But he does it easily. The ball is attached to his foot, too close to allow the defender to take it away from him. Even by his body movements Marcus surprises me. He is light and fast, each step he runs looks like a dance step. Now he is alone with the 'keeper, considering whether to stop and shoot, and from what distance. Finally he decides to shoot while running. A quick right foot is sent forward and the ball goes to the side of the goal near us. Millwall's goalkeeper comes out to the ball and stops. By the shock and panic in his eyes you can understand that it was too close.

All the parents already know Marcus. This is his third season at the academy. Voices of amazement and shock mainly come from me. Following that attack, Marcus decides to get closer to the 'keeper. He puts the defenders surrounding him and the 'keeper no the ground, with a brilliant manoeuvre. The goalkeeper falls to the right, the ball goes slowly to the left and into the net. Even now, except for the satisfaction from the successful move he just performed, Marcus's face doesn't reveal much. The supporters clap and the match goes on. After two attacks, Marcus passes a quick ball over a Millwall defender to another player who is alone; another goal. Only three minutes on the pitch and Marcus was already involved in two goals; scoring the first one and assisting with the other. But don't mention statistics to him, let him play. Now the whole team goes up ahead. Millwall have no answers and shuts themselves up in defence. Goals begin to accumulate. Arsenal do not want to humiliate their rival, after all it is a friendly game, but when Marcus is on the pitch it is not so clear how to avoid it. The Gunners coach decides to move the best player back into defence. He swaps positions, explaining the instructions to his players. Marcus nods 'yes' with his head, and moves downfield. He doesn't really like that position, but again he understands the coach's considerations.

Marcus seems less intimidating in the defence. He's physically inferior and therefore unlikely to be able to physically block the way to the net, or win in one-on-one challenges. Still Marcus is much faster than many rivals. By using his footwork he's forcing them to make mistakes. They lose the ball or pass it over carelessly to another player, allowing a red defender to block the attack. It's already the middle of the second half, and Arsenal are playing fast. The coach decides to change strategy: "Two touches", he instructs his players. He needn't say more, they've been working on this in practice. On first touch the red player gets the ball, on the second he kicks. At first, the match becomes slower. The coach counts: "One, two. Nice Alex", or "One, two, three, Jim! This is one too many touches." Millwall players say thank you and try to catch their breath. A few minutes later the Arsenal players get used to the arrangement, and the match returns to its regular pace. Towards the end Marcus is replaced in order to narrow the gaps between the two teams. He returns to his quiet corner, not too close to the coach, not noticing the parents or the cheering around. He's concentrating on the game, clapping his hands occasionally after an impressive performance.

While Marcus conquers the half pitch of his team, Twinny plays with the second half of the team. Twinny is a blond haired boy with a short spiky haircut, rosy-cheeked with a big captivating smile that never leaves his face. He plays upfront, and when standing or running, or even sitting, it seems that there is a constant aura of charm around him. Twinny is always the first to catch the ball when training starts, he's always chosen by the coach to demonstrate an exercises, and his friends always seek to work in his team. He emits light, but does not overshadow the others. While I was patiently watching Marcus's performance, I occasionally glance to review Twinny's work on the adjacent pitch. Here is Twinny with the ball, shooting from a distance, or passing the ball forward. A scored goal makes him laugh joyfully, call a friend and clap his hands. Millwall's attacking player falls, and Twinny immediately holds out a hand to help him up. Twinny's team is lively, happy, celebrating on the pitch. Twinny especially enjoys getting the ball in the opponent's net, and examine his shooting or passing techniques in front of his rival players. He usually wins these one-on-one contests, so in order for him not to get bored he plays with the ball; he passes it from the left foot to the right and back again, then he deceives the defender to make mistakes using classy moves. After subduing him, he easily scores another striking goal.

Marcus's performance diverted my attention from Twinny, so that when I look his way again, he was no longer on the pitch. Maybe he's sitting on the grass at the substitutes position. Next time I look, Twinny is playing defence. He's not as good in defence. He can't keep up, loses players in one-on-one encounters. Even his aura decreases, and the match is not as happy. I go back to Marcus, and again to Twinny. Now he plays two positions: forward and back. Actually... what's going on here? How can it be? I wonder. Maybe I need a break and some water. Maybe it's too hot today after all.

When the two matches end, all of Arsenal players stand in one row and start their release run together, once towards the parents waiting on the parallel touchlines, and once to the opposite direction. Running is an opportunity for parents to clap and cheer for their hard work. Marcus is too shy. He stood at the end of the line, one before last, clapping his hands gently, but mainly focuses on his release run. In contrast, Dan, his best friend, settles in the middle of the line. He is the tallest one there and his self-confidence adds him a few extra inches. During the run, he takes off his red shirt, waves it over his head in a lasso movement and throws it toward the parents. We all laugh. Dan, who the kids in the academy call 'Beckham' for obvious reasons, enjoys the attention and his ability to entertain an entire crowd. Before he sits down with his team next to the coaches, he runs out of the lines, picks up his shirt and wears it like everyone else. He already feels like a star.

A moment before we sit down, I notice Twinny. Another Twinny standing next to him. The first has an aura and a smile on his face all the time, the second has a small smile nourished from the smile of the Twinny standing next to him. I recognise the proud parents in the crowd.

"Well, you didn't know? Of course they are twins. That's why everyone here call them twins. Adam plays in offence, Terry in defence. They are great kids, are they?"

Jerry

It is not easy being a football player at the academy. Although management is trying to create a positive and pleasant atmosphere during matches and training, and although the children sign an agreement by which they undertake to enjoy academic activities, for some of them the pressure is just too much. Jerry will be ten years old in February. He lives with his parents and younger brother in north London, and this year he was signed to play in Arsenal's academy, after the club's scout saw him playing with friends at school. In honour of the occasion his father bought him new goalkeeping gloves, designed for the most important position on the pitch, at least according to what the goalkeeping coaches at the academy keep saying. His mother told him she was proud of him. Even his little brother wants to be a goalie when he grows up. When Jerry doesn't watch, he tries his new gloves and imagines himself blocking penalties.

The new season, however, did not start well for Jerry. He share the 'keepers position of Arsenal's U10 team with another goalkeeper. In the first two games he got too excited and could not excel himself. This week they play against Chelsea, and he hopes it will be the match that would prove to everyone what he is made of. On Saturday, during the final practice, the coach told them a little about their rivalry with Chelsea. Besides Tottenham, there is no other academy it is so exciting to play against. Jerry already imagines how he manages to stop impossible balls the blue team shoot at him.

It's a rainy Sunday morning. Jerry arrived at the academy with his father and younger brother. They parked their car near the entrance gate because there was no room in the parking lot, and walked the short distance to the dressing room. There, Jerry puts on his yellow shirt with a light baseball cap, to protect his eyes from the sun. That's it – he is ready. Today is the day, he thought, and tried to keep his confidence.

At exactly eleven in the morning he enters the pitch with the rest of his friends. The big pitch is divided in two by the touchlines, six-on-six players from each team in each half. Jerry stood in one of the nets, leaving a small water bottle with the club's crest next to him. His father and little brother stand in the corner position to support him. This is it, now that everything is set, let the referee whistle for the beginning of the match already!

The beginning of the match inspires optimism. Arsenal are better than Chelsea. Little Chris is especially noticeable on the pitch; He breaks the blue team's defence with long balls to the forward players and shoots highballs that mislead them. In the first minutes Chris has already scored two goals for his red team. The Chelsea players don't even get close to Jerry's net. Chris's mother is extremely happy; she came accompanied by her sister and her three nephews. Other parents come to compliment her on her successful son. She stands next to Jerry dad, whose stress is even more evident in light of her rejoicing. "It's not over yet," he shouts at his son, "Look straight" and Jerry looks. On the one hand he's glad Chelsea's attack is not functioning. On the other hand though he is disappointed he hasn't had the chance to prove himself today.

But there, right now, after Chris scores his second goal, an attack is being organised by the blue team. Oh well, not really an attack, just a foolish attempt by one of Chelsea's players to save his team. He takes the ball from midfield, runs alone with it toward the goal, passes across a red defender while the others stand back, not believing their eyes. Now he stands alone with Jerry and hits a too weak shot exactly to the spot the 'keeper is standing in. Jerry almost jumps for joy. The ball is not strong and he knows exactly how to place his arms to pick it up. He threw his arms, grabs the ball with both hands and smiles beneath his peaked cap. Suddenly he feels the ball slips away, and his fingers empty. He hysterically looks down to discover that the ball fell on the grass, just beyond the goal line. Chelsea's players are happy. It's 2–1. If it were up to him, he would bury himself under his peaked cap forever. How did it happen? The ball was already in his hands! He's too embarrassed to look up when he unexpectedly hears his friends encouraged him: "Jerry, nothing happened, everything's fine." His father's voice is also heard calling him: "Lift your head, lift your head." he cries. "It's not over yet."

Three minutes later, he finds himself in the same situation exactly. A different player form Chelsea stands in front of him for a one-on-one. Jerry tries to convince himself that everything would be alright, but the truth is that his hands were shaking a little. He seems obsessed with the ball, trying to guess which way he'll kick it. When he finally did, Jerry jumps, but misses the ball. This time he did not even touch it with his fingertip. It wasn't a hard or particularly a strong ball. Not even close to the posts, in which case he wouldn't stand a chance of catching it. Just a ball, kicked towards his net, without him even touching it. It's 2–2. His team doesn't tell him anything now, except for one who told him to take off the cap that is blocking his vision. Jerry was happy to stay with it, if only to be able to hide his eyes from the piercing looks of others, but he drops it. His father called him from the corner: "It's not over, lift your head", but it seemed to Jerry that his dad's voice was a little lower this time.

The young players of Arsenal's academy continue to dominate the match. Chris kicked some balls towards the goal, though the blue 'keeper blocks them all. A ball kicked by the 'keeper after blocking another shot triggers another attack by Chelsea. This time, the ball was kicked from a distance. Jerry, already without the cap, goes after the ball and grabs it to his chest. He managed to stop it from entering into the net, but the blow was too strong and it drops him to the floor. He lies on his back, one hand is covering his eyes and the other is holding the painful area. And he cries. Not only tears of pain, but out of sadness, out of despair. He can see the image of his dad standing, humiliated, next to Chris's celebrating mother. He cries for his younger brother who also wants to grow up to be a goalkeeper, and because his mother who is waiting for them at home. The gloves dad bought him are now covering his tears, but the excitement can be seen on his rapidly rising and falling belly, at a rate sobbing. His friends don't approach him. They are nervous, without him they could already win. His dad doesn't call him for pep talks from the corner flag, and the coach is withdrawn in the corner. The doctor run towards him, pouring water on his face and asked him if he can continue. He wants to continue, so he wipes his tears and stands up again, without his hat, in the net.

The last five minutes of the match. Arsenal's players keep attacking all the time, but the blue 'keeper stands in the right place. Frustrated Chris begins to kick more strongly but less accurate. His friends in the back are already starting to accept the result. 2–2 is not that awful for a match against Chelsea.

Last minute of the match. A blue player takes the ball, crosses the

Arsenal's exhausted defence and kicks to the net. The ball flies in a bow over Jerry and goes in the net. It's 3–2 to Chelsea. The players celebrate, and the referee blows his whistle to mark the end of the game.

Jerry sits down on the grass, unable to find the strength to get up. His players, with their heads humiliated, go together to the dressing room, not even trying to keep their voices down while asking for the head of the 'keeper. Parents are left to wait for them on the lines. What are they saying to his father now? And how does he manage to look them in the eye? Jerry doesn't know how, and he's afraid to ask. After the pitch empties out he passes asks his father to take him home. Together they make the long journey to the vehicle parked at the gate. As they pass the driveway, he feels everyone is pointing at him. He wears a hat and hides his eyes. At school he was the star of the team, a local hero. Here he can't even keep the ball and made his team lose the important match against Chelsea. What did he need it for? And why did his father have to park so far away?

Winter, a time for new beginnings

Arsenal training

Jerry did not stay at the academy. He could not withstand the pressure that his position requires. From his team's game against Chelsea, Jerry mainly remembers his father standing embarrassed compared to Chris's mother's Joyful cheers. He also couldn't erase from his memory the insulted eyes of his brother, who also dreamed of becoming a goalkeeper. That's why the academy did not encourage parental involvement in children games. During special classes at the academy the parents learn the importance of encouraging their son at all times, along with the damage caused by the use of psychological pressure. Parents who do not meet the code of behaviour are exceptions. Parents often exhibit a friendly spirit, even playfulness, as they stand on the sidelines.

Instead of Jerry, two new goalkeepers joined the U10 Arsenal team: Ron and Cody. Ron looks small relative to his other friends, Cody is much larger physically. Both are under ten, and they have a lot to prove. The concluding training before the match on Saturday is a good opportunity.

Training takes place in the Dome, the academy's indoor pitch. It rains outside and the wind threatens to pull the trees out of the ground. Ron and Cody, who usually trains on the goalkeepers open pitch, got approval to be together with their team today in the closed pitch. First they practice on the side with the goalkeeper's coach. The second part of the training is a six on six match on a size half-pitch, a good opportunity for both young 'keepers to show what they have to offer. Before the opening whistle of the match everyone, including Ron and Cody, shake hands, even though they were practicing together during the last hour. Cody is standing at the net nearest to me, Ron in distant one.

Ron's parents did not to come watch practice today. Ron didn't seem to mind. Despite his slim figure he is upright and secure, completely controlling everything and everyone standing in his small and un-marked space. He easily stops the first shots kicked at him and makes the crowd whistle with enthusiasm. He doesn't pay attention to them. The boundaries of his mind are now the boundaries of this small pitch, and beyond that he does not see or hear anything. When his friends go out for an attack he leaves his goal with security, almost joining them. When one of his friends does something good, he applauds him. When someone makes a less successful move, he shakes his head right and left, as if to say 'no'. His performance is reminiscent of a theatrical performance; it's measured and staged. As if he saw countless football broadcasts, and is now applying exactly the same small movements made by the best goalkeepers in the world.

Cody, however, is much more relaxed. He leaves the show to his dad, who enters the Dome proud, tall and confident just as the match begins. Cody's father is at least two heads high compared to other parents watching the match, and at least twice as loud as them. When he entered the hall, no one can took his eyes off of him, and he is immediately surrounded with a happy, noisy crowd. All his 'gang' stands to the left of the goal. At first, they did not manage to attract Cody's attention, but when the father comes into action, he smiles and replies. The dialogue between them goes something like this:

Father: "Cody, how ugly you are. And you are a really terrible goalkeeper!"

Cody reveals two heart captivating dimples smiling and shaking his head up and down and back. The father continues: "How did I get such an ugly kid? Cody, you look nothing like your dad. You left all the beauty to me. And I beat you in football as well, you know. You will never be a good goalie like your old man!"

Cody: "I know, I know."

Father: "Who is the most handsome?"

Cody: "You."

Father: "And who's the best player?"

Cody: "You."

Meanwhile, the attack is approaching Cody's goal. A long shot to the middle of the goal, and Cody does not push the ball strong enough. Another kick to the goalpost, and Cody jumps and pushes aside. The attack ends without a goal, thanks to the last man on the defence line. Cody's father, noisy even more than before, begins to sing: "This is my son, this is my son. Great goalkeeper, but still ugly!" The mood on the pitch is joyful and bouncy. Almost everyone joins the celebration. Even Cody, who is trying to stay focused on the match, hits a little dance.

Meanwhile there is an attack on the other side. Serious Ron frowns at the ball, and the ball, as if out of fear, loses the momentum as it approaches the goalpost. Ron stops this ball easily. Unfortunately his team is much less offensive and defensive than the rival team, and more shots are kicked over to Ron. He manages to stop all the shots in the first half but in the second, he starts taking balls out from the net. One, two, three. I begin to worry for him. The fourth goal is scored by a young defender from a rebound after Ron runs to the ball and gets it in the stomach. The young 'keeper lies down on the Dome synthetic grass and doesn't get up. For a moment, pictures from Jerry's fall cross my mind. The one that made him lie down on his back in heart-breaking cry. But Ron doesn't cry. A few more moments and he's back on his feet, tall and proud as before, stands in striking confidence on the goal line. I can't help but wonder: what a remarkable mental strength for a ten-year-old child!

On the other side Cody and his dad continue with the show. Throughout the match Cody concedes only one goal. Not so because of his extraordinary abilities, mainly because of the weakness of the opposing team. This does not prevent them from celebrating. When the coach whistles to the end of training, Cody crosses the touchline to hug his father. Now the father provides the encore, and loudly declares: "Do not touch me. You're on fire! Cody, you're so hot, I'm afraid to get burned!" Cody smiles with his dimples glowing with happiness. Ron is not as happy while walking from the pitch, but he's proud. He's getting pats on the back from their coach and from parents. Four goals in one half is a lot, but it's just training, and he will have more opportunities to prove himself when it really matters. Maybe even in tomorrow's match.

Just before everyone goes home, the coach receives a phone call with bad news. The match supposed to take place tomorrow against Ipswich was postponed due to unfavourable weather conditions. This message of course, makes all the team players sad, but for Ron, it's even sadder. He gets off the pitch with his head down. This sadness of his, however, unlike Jerry's melancholy from only a few weeks ago, is sadness coming from anticipation to the next match.

A week later, it's still rainy and cold; I join the practice in the same hall. Three coaches are going around thirty players who are divided into two teams. In order not to waste time on pitch arrangement, they pre-divide the pitch into four, with different training accessories waiting in each part. In a quarter to ten the coaches gather the kids in a semicircle and explain the exercises. At ten exactly, they begin a continuous ninety minutes training. The topic of today training is headers. The coaches explain, demonstrate and practice. "A header can come from different places, some balls are high, some low and some flat. When it's a high ball, the head must be set to the highest point of the ball, so that he would land downwards instead of fly to such heights, where you have no control over it." The coach demonstrates the coordination exercise with twin Adam, or as everyone calls him here, Twinny. He throws him a ball at different heights and Twinny heads the ball according to the explanations. When he's done, everyone gets up to practice the headers. The tempo increases in the next exercise. Now the kids are asked to head the ball while interrupted and in a limited time frame. One, two, run and head the ball. The cheering changes between "Good job" and "bad luck", "Think faster" and "Good response!"

All exercises end at eleven and a short practice match begins. Both teams shake hands, grab their spots, and the coach whistles for the beginning of the game. "Practice headers," he asks, and the kids are trying to apply the techniques they have just been practicing for the last hour, this time under playing conditions. The children are having a hard time but they don't give up. The coach flatters all of them.

At half past eleven the children gather in the corner of the hall for a summary talk. The coaches instil them with motivation; "We have a match tomorrow. Use it to practice what you have learned in training during the week. Don't be lazy, try to practice the skills. Remember, you are part of the glorious Arsenal Football Club. If you want to be here, show it!" And loudly for all to hear, they add: "Good job, boys. Good job!"

Chelsea v Ipswich

The following week, the Chelsea's academy is playing against Ipswich. It's a freezing Sunday at the Chelsea's training ground; It's Rainy and windy, dark clouds are in the sky. The wide grass areas are all around us, and there is no building in sight to block the wind. Chelsea's U10 team is playing against Ipswich's U10s; Chelsea's have more economic resources. Its players look stronger, faster and better trained.

Despite the alleged superiority of the blue players, Ipswich's number nine player is the one who catches my eye. He is small, thin, but in great shape; He doesn't stop running for a moment, and when the ball is far out, he hops over some hurdles and reaches it as fast as he can. He has no time, he has an excellent football team to beat. His cheeks are rosy from the cold and effort, but it seems he does not feel anything. He's here to play football.

His friends also want to win, but they are not as capable as him. Right next to me stands Roy's father, who is playing for Ipswich defence. It's not an easy task to be the last to separate between Chelsea's attacking players and the net, and little Roy's odds are fifty-fifty. On each ball he manages to push away, there is one that eludes him. It is already 2–0 in Chelsea's favour by half-time. When the players leave the pitch to take the half-time break, Roy father explains: "It's only football. It's a simple game. But the players of Ipswich are so afraid of the name that they can't even play. My son would never miss these simple shots if the players in front of him were not wearing these blue shirts."

The second half opening was better for Roy and his friends, and during the next thirty minutes they manage not to concede a goal. Their defence is doing a good job, but the attack is a bit tired. After Roy manages to rescue the ball from Chelsea's attacking player, he delivers a beautiful one-touch shot. His father, standing next to me, screams out of joy: "Yes, this is football! See? This is football. Simple. Just Football!" The fact that this last attack ends without scoring, does not subdue his excitement. In the final minutes of the match Chelsea's young players manage to score two more goals into the underdog's net, and the final result is 4–1 for the blue team. Just before Roy dad goes to wait for his son outside the changing room, he said: "Well, we lost. But at least it was a good match. In the second half they started to play football… at least we played football," he concludes and keeps on walking, deep in thoughts, toward the building.

When the match ends, we join the big pitch to witness the U14's play. One of the parents told us that the result is already 4–0 in favour of Ipswich. Chelsea's U10 coach stands on the pitch's touchline. He is in good mood, and the result doesn't bother him. "Come on Boys, come on Chelsea," he calls, and continues telling his academy jokes parade. Parents standing beside him are in the amused audience, which he needs on order to continue with the performance. A few minutes later, when he sees the blue team continues to play defensively, he gives up. "They don't even play football. You can lose, it's not a shame. But at least play football!" He calls at us, and then leaves.

Scott Sinclair

Six months after I began compiling a list of names of potential players in my notebook, I open it again with great excitement. Seven names who might be stars one day are listed. But now, in this late hour of the evening, I will not add it another name. This time, in the excitement of a first time, because this is indeed the first time, I mark a victory sign next to the name: number eleven, Scott, reserve team, Chelsea.

At the beginning of this season Scott Sinclair is picked for the first time and on a regular basis for Chelsea's first team. He thus became the first player moving to play with the first team since the club's academy went through its reorganisation and adjusted to the current management system. A framed picture of him, running on the pitch with the ball between his feet, wearing a blue shirt with the number 11 printed on it, was already hanging in the academy. The number of years he trained at the academy, as well as the name of the club he is now playing with, are listed in the caption below: 'Chelsea Football Club.' Two hundred players who dream of making the exact same path from the academy to the first eleven of the glorious football club look at this picture every day. The academy coaches are now serving pints of beer to celebrate the event. Many months will pass until someone can wipe the smiles off their faces when someone mentions Sinclair's name.

On the evening of 23 September, a few weeks after the start of the league's new season, Sinclair is for the first time, in the starting line-up of the Cup match against Hull City from the Second league. Chelsea is guided by its new manager standing on the lines, Avram Grant. They win this match against this professionally inferior rival 2–0. Scott scores one of these goals, adding a line to his academic history, as well as his own. Sinclair is the first player out of Chelsea's academy since its reorganisation; the first to be in the opening eleven, and the first to score a goal for the first team already in this match. He will have many more challenges to cross. During that season, he will be lent to a club from the second division, return to play with Chelsea's first team, then lent again to the end of the season. A long period will pass until he'll be able to wear the blue and white kit again. During this period, he will play in matches in which he will receive the ball match as a reward for scoring three goals, along with matches where he will be less noticeable. He will play for Swansea City and for Manchester City, finally (for now) he will sign a contract in Aston Villa in 2015. A bright future is still ahead for this nice young lad. In his first mission, Sinclair has succeeded. Just as he opened in the match, he scored a goal for the first team of the academy in which he was raised. No matter to which club he will be lent in the future, he will always be a Chelsea's player first. Personally, I believe that Scott Sinclair will successfully pass through all of the obstacles and will finally be a successful Premier League player. I even have a small notebook in which his name is written in, to prove it.

It's Christmas time

Lower league football

The Christmas vacation in the academies gives me time to test new and additional arenas of English football. On Christmas Eve black-and-white films were broadcasted on TV. A wave of sweet nostalgia urged me to go and find the authentic English football, people are always busy praising what was allegedly here prior to the big money, the foreigners and the media; the same old homely, embracing football from the neighbourhood.

I started the new adventure at a League One match of Leyton Orient against Gillingham at the Brisbane Road stadium, on a particularly cold Tuesday. The news promised special snow but in the end it was just commonplace rain that wets your trousers and makes your toes freeze. An hour before the match I'm standing in a long line of residents from a greyish London neighbourhood, their toes are frozen as well. While waiting, you can observe the changes made in the neighbourhood after the renovation of the new complex of the local football club. A community centre was built on one side of the road with the football club's symbol on its top. This is a new building, brilliant, and its walls are made of glass. The college is located next to it. A synthetic grassy area is located in its centre on to which you can't enter without the correct shoes.

On the other side of the road, adjacent to the hidden stadium is a line of completely new multi-stories buildings, the club offices and some too-expensive souvenir shops are located. A giant symbol of the club is towering over everything, and the bright red colours conceal any sense of grayness, that might have characterised in the past the neighbourhood that is represented by the club. For a moment, I think we got confused; is that what a stadium of a club in the third tier looks like? They are asking for twenty pounds for a single ticket. Leyton Orient ranks in seventh place in the third division. Their opponent Gillingham, are ranked in seventeenth place. This is a mid-table match, which is likely not to change anything in each of the clubs fortunes. From this I conclude that the relatively high amount I was going to spend during the next two hours are not due to the quality of the match that is going to take place soon on the pitch. Anyway, I'm too cold to ask questions.

My ticket takes me to a seat in the stand behind the goal. More than six thousand and five hundred other supporters place their bottoms in the marked seats. A family sits to my left: a father, mother and three tiny blond children. They are talking and laughing among themselves, sharing different snacks. The mother sitting next to me gets a small box of Pringles. The players' entrance to the pitch is accompanied by a cheerful announcement: "Welcome your home team, Leyton Orient!" the audience responds by indifferent applauses. The hands of the mother are busy with her box of Pringles so she doesn't join the quiet chorus. A few minutes into the match she closes the box, puts it aside and wipes her hands with a wet wipe she pulls out of her bag. Then she cleans her children's hands and hands one wipe to the father. The whole family is busy with their snacks and with themselves; they hardly take a minute to watch the match. The truth is that there is not much to see. Among the home team there is one player, Paul Terry, whose name is possibly familiar to you because of his younger brother, John, who plays for the blue team of the city centre. His family lineage is currently the only attraction on the pitch. Towards the 80-minute point of the match, the parents and their three children leave the stand without waiting to see what the outcome will be.

The local team's match is most probably just an occasion, an excuse to spend the day together. Otherwise it's quite impossible to comprehend what makes six thousand spectators watch this boring game for ninety minutes. The team's gathering area give a festive feeling and the clean, comfy pitch as well as the cheerful announcers voice, stick around, even after both gloomy teams start to play as well as after they leave the pitch. Besides, there's Pringles and the conversation which they started with the children during breakfast, can be continued. When it's done, they wipe their hands from crisps leftovers and go home early. The match ends in the miserable result of a 0–0. After I check the results of the rest of the weekend's games on the TV at the snack bar, which serves only non-fried food, I go home. I wish I had come out of the stadium a few minutes before the match ended, I could have avoided the traffic.

It's Saturday in at Valley Stadium. An FA Cup match between Charlton and West Bromwich Albion. It is the oldest competition in England and as a matter of fact, in the world. With an expression of historical legacy on my face, I make my way from north London all the way to Charlton located in the south of the city. I met Ali on the train; A nice girl with a red scarf of the home team. Across from her sits a father with his son, West Bromwich supporters, with their blue scarves. Charlton is currently ranked in sixth place of the second division, whereas West Bromwich in ranked first. According to the hard data, this match is expected to be intense and full of emotions. They used to say that you could measure rivalries according to the temperature, produced by the supporters of both teams in the railroad car going to the match. Then again the only emotion we have seen around is expressed in soft whisperings, aimed not to disturb other passengers in the car; supporters sitting next to us are meanwhile discussing the second league table, then they continue with book reviews.

Charlton's Valley Stadium is impressively beautiful. Although it's not as fancy as the other new stadiums in north London, but the renovations it went through five years ago made it happy, colourful and welcoming. As the name implies, the stadium is in a Valley, which is the lowest spot in the neighbourhood. The parade of people walking there feels like a flowing river. When you get in the neighbourhood and look around, you can't help but feeling the stadium is like a pearl in a stack of hay; A centre of prestige in the landscape. The inside design of the stadium is reminiscent of Premier League stadiums. A large electronic screen displays the team's players and some admirable track records. The perfect sound system is playing grandiose music from different adventure movies. A moment before presenting the players, I am positive Russell Crowe in his gladiator costume is going to march onto the pitch any minute now. I can almost see him walk in to the sound of stamping feet made by the raging crowd in the Colosseum.

No kidding, the player's presentation is no less theatrical than that. The amusing announcer suddenly calls to all ten thousand spectators "Welcome to the Valley! This is Charlton!" He emphasized each word and gives each vowel its place of honour. Perfect production. It actually works; after watching as a neutral for three minutes, I realise I just adopted myself a team from the Second Division. And it's not because they play good football.

This match might be better than the one from five days ago, but it is not so great here also. Despite of the goal Charlton scores during the first minute, the match reaches new heights of boredom and ends in a disappointing 1–1 result, ensuring a replay. Neither West Bromwich nor Charlton have shown any potential that could help them get promoted to the Premier League at the end of this season. I have a long drive home, and plenty of time to get my tickets to watch some beautiful football of the Premier League.

The movie special played on Christmas Eve was different this time. It was interesting, fascinating and managed to keep me awake in front of the screen for long hours. When I returned home from the Valley after the match, I zapped back and forth among the TV channels and thought to myself that sometimes we learn to appreciate the old things only when we know, without a doubt, that tomorrow we will get the new thing back. Not much was left from the community working-class football. As times passes by, nostalgia is painting the past with bright colours. Leyton Orient supporters pay twenty pounds for a ticket not just to watch football; they come to enjoy the experience. Maybe sometimes they miss the authentic football that was here thirty years ago; feeling the warmth, the closeness and the smell of men's sweat on the terracing. Do they really hope for the return of working class football? I am not sure. My opinion is that longing for the past is a privilege only those who live in the present have. And in the present they can come here with their children and tell them about great past stories while sitting at ease in the families stands.

Arsenal v Charlton

It is a pleasant sunny day, and Arsenal's Academy are playing against Charlton's academy. The grass is still wet from the rain that fell during the night and my feet are frozen, but the sun in the sky warms my heart. The academy players returned from the Christmas holidays this week feeling energised and hungry and the match on the pitch is fast and ambitious. Almost instinctively, I stand up to watch the U10 match, again. At the beginning of the second half, the score is already 3–0 in favour of the

Gunners. Arsenal are playing well. The players take pleasure in what apparently seems as simple passes of the ball; while one player receives the ball, he jumps over it, leaving it to the player standing behind him. They repeat this exercise again and again while embarrassing Charlton's defence a bit more each time. One of these manoeuvres resulted in a goal. Little Timothy receives one of these balls but instead of kicking it, he runs forward. The net is located to his right and his left leg is kicking a long ball at a sharp angle. The 'keeper blocks the right corner, but the ball went right to the left. An additional Arsenal attacking player, who is not sure whether the ball is going to hit the net or go out, adds a small touch which will undoubtedly credit the home team with another goal. Timothy is annoyed. He turns to the player who last touched the ball in a louder voice than he intended: "This is my goal. It was mine even if you didn't touch it!" His teammate doesn't respond. The parents standing on the goal line are giggling; their giggles reveal deep embarrassment. Timothy receives some cold stares even from the bench. He is rather embarrassed. He didn't mean to barge in this way. While passing by his coach, he says nothing and only looks down to the grass. The next time Timothy gets a ball and scores, he doesn't celebrate, but only claps his hands twice over his head to honour the players who contributed to the attack. Towards the end of the match he receives the ball in a convenient position. It's a one-on-one against the 'keeper, while the corner closest to him is protected. He passes the ball to a player on his right, who scores another goal. Timothy smiles with relief. His mistake is forgiven.

At the same time, another drama is taking place on the pitch. Mark usually plays in midfield. Today he was assigned to the left and the truth is he doesn't really know what to do in this position. As if he needs more pressure, his family also came to watch him; His father, mother and two brothers who are standing exactly along the line on which he's supposed to play. On every opportunity they throw comments at him: "play on the line, Mark!" "Take this ball!" "Kick it!" And Mark, as if on purpose, fails these missions one after the other. Towards the end of the match his family members are so desperate, that they finally cease to call him. Although his team wins, his performance was bad. One of the other mothers approaches Mark's family to ask how they were. Mark's sixteen-year-old brother is happy to find an open ear for his complaints; "They put him in the wrong position today. He couldn't function. We don't know what to do…"

"Do not worry," the lady assures her. "My son is also not used to play the position he was assigned to today. Nevertheless, I'm happy that the coach made this change. This way the kids learn about themselves and about the match. That's the way to learn football".

The manner in which the parents and their kids grasp the events on the pitch is a matter of attitude. Nonetheless, attitude is not something you are born with, just as violent football isn't. Both are the result of education. Education of the supporters, the academy football players and their parents. "A positive approach to the match is the basic feature we look for in children that we want to sign," I was told by one of the academies managers. "Physical skills are essential, but you just cannot train, qualify or teach a child that has no positive approach to the match, no matter how talented he is". The attitude the child brings from his home is reinforced in the academies in different ways.

When Timothy snapped at his teammate, no one was angry with him, nor did they reprimand him. Still, by seeing the parents' stares and feeling their embarrassment, he realized his behaviour wasn't appropriate. He will try to make amends for his mistake. Timothy's embarrassment indicates that he understood the ideals upon which the match should be played. The coach and the parents didn't have to say anything.

Even the parent's behaviour on the sidelines is the result of supportive educational and a non-destructive approach. As requested, the parents convey confidence and support by clapping and cheers. When Cody and his dad behave foolishly during training by telling jokes and dancing around, they are implementing the silent principles of the academy; Enjoy, create a friendly, stress-free atmosphere.

Each moment in the academy is organised to the smallest details, even when it appears spontaneous. The event is designed as a pleasant, friendly experience, free of stress. Even when there is reason to be nervous or angry, a person who will relieve the atmosphere will be found; When Mark's family shows impatience and anger regarding their son's position, as we've just seen, one of the mothers approached them, and in a casual conversation, she explained the rationale behind the coaches' action. "My son is also not used to play the position he was assigned to today. Nevertheless, I'm happy. That's the way to learn football."

David's difficult loan

On Sabbath dinner at Johnny's parents, Roy, the youngest, and David, his best friend keep me up to date with all their stories. As agreed with Arsenal's academy, David finally moved to the north of England and played for a third division football club. Roy didn't join him. He actually wanted to, but he had to finish school, and to continue the training period as a youth coach.

"David will be able to visit us whenever he's in town," his mother comforts him.

"It's just for one season," his father tries. "Next year he'll come back here and play with Arsenal. You'll see, he might even arrange some discounted tickets to the Emirates Stadium!"

And Johnny? He thought it's possible to make a great film out of this drama, even if films about footballers are so corny.

Roy had a hard time at first, but as time passed, he devoted himself to his work and found comfort. During the next few months, David didn't come to London, nor did he visit the families' house on Fridays. Life as a professional player is different to his academic life, and he was committed to a busy schedule, especially on weekends. David missed Roy and Johnny's family, and the family missed him. In the meantime we all followed his progress through the daily papers that report all matches in the professional leagues. During dinners, Roy would tell us about David's last week trainings in detail, and about the goal he assisted on Saturday. In case I missed the Sabbath dinner, Johnny would fill me in these stories.

The period after the departure of David to the distant city was traumatic. Indeed Arsenal did everything they could to help him, but there are things that simply were not under their control. David's parents were forced to leave their jobs for a period of several months, and the distance from Spain created problems with the little brothers. When his parents returned to their homeland, and David was left alone, he began being lazy with cooking and taking care of himself. He ate mostly fast food and suffered from poor hygiene. The northern accent was also hard for him, and he didn't integrate with the team. The coach couldn't turn the eleven players into a functional unit on the pitch. In addition to all of that, the club has encountered some financial difficulties that created an unpleasant atmosphere in the dressing rooms. Eight games after the opening of the season, and the David's team was already below the red line.

In addition to everything else, one evening David felt severe pain in his stomach. He tried to ignore it, he didn't want to lose the match scheduled for tomorrow, so he went to bed early. He woke up the next morning sweating and suffering. He managed to call the director of the Arsenal academy while he's in the worst pain he ever felt in all the years of his life. After a couple of long distance phone calls, David was rushed to the hospital. He turned out to be suffering from food poisoning, probably the result of the bad food he grabbed on the way home. While feeling lonely, suffering and not understanding a word of this northern English around him, he was hospitalised for three whole days, and decided he had enough. He wants to return home to Spain. Even after recovering, he still wasn't able to get back to his former shape. His skills, which were praised by Arsene Wenger only a few months ago, had dropped drastically.

Throughout David's' loan period, Arsenal academy coaches did not remove him from their responsibility. Once every few weeks they would go to visit him and watched the matches in which he participated. When he was in the hospital one of the coaches came to visit him regularly, brought him food, and mainly offered comfort. When he recovered and returned to practice, the coaches uploaded videos from every minute of his match to his private Website. At first they were short films; Three minutes as a substitute in the first match, two and a half minutes in a second. They had long phone conversations with him every week; they reminded him of his skills from the last academy season and encouraged him to improve his left foot. "Even Wenger is following you", they told him. "You are not alone." David's physical health as well as his mood began improving gradually. We heard him on the speaker during a telephone conversation with Roy, while we were having our customary dinner. He already sounded calmer, more self-confident.

"It's a challenge, and I know that I have the strength to get through it", he said. The improvement in his mood also affected his performance on the pitch. He gradually got more minutes on the pitch, and in one of the matches, he even made it to the opening lineup! His name began appearing in football reports more frequently, and the goals he scored were forever preserved in the newspapers. Even Roy's mood gradually improved as his good friend was doing better, and dinner conversations have become so much more lively and happy.

Building an empire

The Emirates stadium

"Today we have two new signings of two talented young boys. The first is..." Andy turns to the small boy on the left, and asks him in which position he plays. The toddler replies that he plays as a left-back. Andy is excited: "How nice, we just need one. And how much money you want to earn in a week?" The boy thinks for a moment, and looks sheepishly at his father and then quickly ejects: "Ten thousand pounds." Andy: "We have a left-back here, a little expensive, but I believe we'll manage. And you?" Andy turns to the second one. The latter replies: "striker." Andy seems a bit disappointed. "Ah, another striker... Oh, well. And how much you want to earn a week?"

After they agree on a salary of forty thousand pounds, Andy signs the two children on some forms, takes out two small bottles that 'players drink', and concludes in the following sentence: "Just so you know, from this moment on I am your agent and I get 95 percent commission. Okay with you?" The boys nod joyfully.

***

One of the rooms in the new Emirates Stadium of Arsenal FC is a museum that tells and presents the club's history. Arsenal's museum is not big and cannot contain a lot of people. Roughly estimated, no more than forty. The design is most impressive; Carpeted floor, moving pictures, voices from old matches playing on the sound system. It's a performance of light, sound and colour. Two statues of the club founders are positioned at the museum entrance. A white caption written on a red background quotes one of them, Herbert Chapman, as he said in 1925: "I am going to make this the greatest club in the world", The big symbol of the club displayed next to it gives the impression that this statement is not too far from being true.

The museum presents the club's achievements over the years. Some are restored; from some there are pictures and videos. Flags of all clubs who competed against Arsenal over the years, as well as trophies and medals are displayed behind glass covered cabinets. Large full size photographs of international players are hanged on the walls. Images of former esteemed players are changing on a TV screen above. In one of the corners there is a statue of Charlie George, known as Charlie Boy, as he lay on the pitch, just after he scored the winning goal in the FA Cup Final against Liverpool at Wembley Stadium. This was a dramatic goal, scored during extra-time which set the final score of the match against Merseysider's glory club. That same end result, 2–1 for the Gunners, granted them the trophy and completed a double for the club during the 1970/71 season. The statue of Charlie Boy lying, arms aloft in triumph, returns the viewer to that same wonderful moment that entered the gold pantheon of the history of the club. George, by the way, is currently employed in the club's hospitality department.

For the small children, the museum planners created a number of captivating computer games about the history of Arsenal. Computer games are colourful, fast and loud, perfectly suitable for the young children temperaments. The games are designed not to be too difficult so that everyone could enjoy. Knowledge is not the thing here, the experience of the visitor is, and the feeling is that he, as a supporter, is a part of this magnificent club as well.

Tours around the new stadium go out regularly several times a day from the museum. Asmhar, a confirmed Arsenal supporter, was our guide. The tour started in one of the directors' entrances. The wall at the entrance is made of Marble; Asmhar explains that the material was chosen because the directors' stand in the legendary Highbury Stadium in which the club played before moving to the Emirates stadium, was also made of marble. Two photographs are hanging in the same entrance: the first is from the last match at Highbury; the second from the first match at the Emirates.

Three main goals have guided the design of the new building. The first was to create an enthusiastic atmosphere of encouragement during the matches. For this purpose, the pitch was located close to the stands, with no barriers or separating jogging tracks. Between the supporters sitting in the front row and their gods playing on the pitch, are just advertising signs, 25 inches tall. The stadium roof is also designed and built in a unique fashion meant to provide acoustic support to the sounds of encouragement. Every little noise in the stadium is loudly heard, and the cheering voices of dozens of supporters sounds as if there were made by hundreds of thousands.

The quality of the grass is the second goal. To do so, they built a transparent roof above the pitch, allowing sunlight to penetrate. Four vents placed in each corner of the pitch, as in Highbury stadium, are also used for the same purpose. "Circulation", Asmhar explains "Is our secret. We have the best pitch in England". The natural grass is covered with a special material that keeps it. Except for the Arsenal team players, the away team and the referees, there are only five people in the UK that have permission to get on the pitch. They are all groundsmen, of course.

The ongoing care of the stadium's grass is done from both directions. From above – special lamps heat the grass on cold winter days. From its bottom there is a special underground system, which function is to balance the temperature. It heats the surface when it snows, while when it's wet, it dries and absorbs the rain. Apart from growing trees of money, this system does everything. The stadium is also 'green'; Rainwater is collected for reuse for irrigation. He doesn't forget to tell us about the hawk that arrives every morning to ward off pigeons seeking to leave their wastes on the pitch. "That's an old trick," Asmhar assures us, when he sees the doubtful looks in our eyes, "they already used it for many years at airports".

The third cause, and perhaps the most important of all is to create an experience of convenience for the supporters. All the seats at the Emirates Stadium are padded with comfortable fabric, supporting the supporters' bottoms during the long sitting periods. Even when supporters get up from their seats (when goals are scored in favour of the home team), you can't hear all sixty thousand seats close at the same time. The stadium is also optimised for supporters with disabilities: for the blind, special hand rails were places to match their walking sticks and outside the stadium, they even built lavatories for Guide Dogs! People with walking difficulties receive, when they get their season ticket, a parking space in the stadium as well as special places for those in wheelchairs.

Restaurants and cafés were opened in the directors' stands and one of them even holds one Michelin star. Hot and cold drinks are served to supporters in the stands upon their exit at half-time. There are also four large ballrooms for conferences and celebrations in the Emirates Stadium.

The demand, in case you're interested, exceeds the supply; it turns out that many young lovers choose to get married in halls in which the football club's symbol is stamped on each of the chair. During summer vacations stadium is also leased for large outdoor events, such as Brazil's national team matches and music shows.

Hundred and twenty thousand tourists come to tour the Emirates every year; each of them pays a modest entrance fee. These are the supporters, athletes and business people who wish to learn from the economic and social success of the football club. They finish the tour in the gift shop located at the entrance to the venue. This store offers different goods; starting with kits, underwear and bathrobes, through school products and dog bowls, to books, games and CDs, all stamped with the club's crest, of course. In the exit of the gift shop there is a sign hanging that says: "Goodbye. See you again. You're the twelfth man and make the difference. Thank you for your support. Come on you Gunners!' This sign is doing exactly what every detail in the stadium design manages to do: to sponsor, on the one hand, the high financial costs of construction and maintenance of a stadium with sixty thousand seats, and on the other hand, to create a feeling of bond between the supporters and their adored team.

Stamford Bridge

It's just a weekday in a completely ordinary week, late in the morning. Fifteen people are already standing in line for the organised tour of the Stamford Bridge Stadium, each of whom paid fifteen pounds to join. In a few minutes, when we'll walk together to the first exhibition room we will be almost thirty strong. Meanwhile, Andy, our guide, is smiling at newcomers and gives each one a necklace with a large pendant decorated with a Chelsea's crest. There is something rather symbolic in wearing this pendant; the shoulders align a little and the look in the eyes becomes more determined. Although we are only occasional tourists, guests for a moment, in this moment we too belong to the great and glorious club and here we have a pendant around our necks to prove it.

At quarter past two we enter the first display room together. The European Cup is displayed on our left. To our right, stands a podium with the club's biggest players behind it. "You can take as many pictures as you like", guide Andy invites us. He understands exactly what the meaning of a picture is on the blue podium, with Chelsea's all-time greatest players in the background. It is a life altering moment, particularly for young children. The picture session takes a few minutes, then Andy asks whether we are all Chelsea supporters. Twenty-seven of us answer yes. Two brave ones reveal their sympathy towards another club, the first to Liverpool, and the second, an Italian tourist is an Inter Milan supporter. Quietly, Andy wishes the Italian supporter good luck, as his team plays against Liverpool in the round of 16 of Champions League Cup Final soon.

On our way to the next showroom we pass behind the stands of the stadium, the snack bars and public restrooms are just next to us. We are close to each other all the time, stepping forward with determination. Cheering songs dedicated to the team are coming out of the speakers, and for the sake of variation, cries of excitement and long shouts of joy are heard from time to time. The walk is not short, but exciting. It manages to convey precisely the experience of forty thousand supporters cheering in the stands during a match. The next place we come to is the media room, which convened a press conference at the end of each match. There is a small kitchenette, bar, two TV screens and a position for journalists to place their PCs. A table and a few chairs are placed in the centre. Andy takes the middle chair and seats two little ones next to him. It's show time.

"This table has a lot of history. It is the table on which the biggest players of Chelsea were signed in recent years, including Ruud Gullit and Gianfranco Zola. At this table sat Mourinho when he said: "I am the special one". Andy makes a funny imitation of the Blues legendary manager. "Some of the biggest signings of our club have been made here. Who is your favourite player?" Andy turns to the older one of two young children sitting to his right: "John Terry", he replies. "At this table exactly where you are sitting now, sat John Terry when he signed his contract with Chelsea". The boy is excited, and Andy continues with his show. He turns to us, the audience, while we are sitting on the reporter seats, saying: "Today we have two new signings". And here comes the amusing signing ceremony described earlier in this chapter. When it ends, Andy and the kiddos vacate the table for more supporters who dream of signing a contract of millions with Chelsea on this table.

Then we go to the changing room and pass through a small interview room on the way. Andy tells us that it's called 'Lampard's room', "because after every match they interview the best player here". The dressing rooms of the away team are relatively modest, they are built in a 'tactical' manner: lockers, for example, are placed under the seats, so that when visiting players bend to put their things, their backs will be strained; Andy is joking, off course, or so I hope. The hangers are low so that when they stand up, they will get hit in the head; and the tactics board is hanging behind the door, only that it must remain open most of the time, so the players can hardly see the moves painted by the manager.

The home teams dressing room is large, luxurious and much better equipped. Each player has a locker bearing his name. Between the cupboards there is a TV screen playing big moments from Chelsea matches, to motivate the players before going out fir the match. The massage room is on the side, with five beds in it. Andy tells that Terry usually lies first since he is the captain and he likes to see anyone who comes into the locker room. Frankie lies second because he's Frankie, and all the rest share the other three beds. The medical staff in the stadium is well equipment and have the ability to handle a wide range of injuries, including broken ribs. In the worst case there is a hospital nearby. There is a briefings board in one of the side rooms, where the players get instructions for the game. It also contains ten small showers and a small rubber bath designated for used as an ice bath.

From there we go to the tunnel. Before heading onto the pitch Andy tries to give us the feeling that we are players in two teams, about to go onto the pitch to the sound of the roar of forty thousand supporters. He asks Chelsea supporters to stand on the right side of the tunnel, and those who are not, meaning the supporters of Liverpool and Inter supporter, on the left. "You are Chelsea," he said to the first team. "And you Liverpool," he said to the other. "Everybody ready? Come on". And so we leave the tunnel. Some of us touch the Chelsea sign placed just before the tunnel's exit, as part of the tradition of the English players. Even if the stands were full at the moment, I think that some of us could not get any more excited than that. The home bench is on our left, and on the right is that of the visitors. "Here sat the special one in the past", Andy says, pointing at the managers' chair with awe of respect. The children, who want to be photographed sitting on the chair, feel no less special.

Box number four in the stand in front of the seats, is the only box where the chairs are not marked. There sits the club owner, Roman Abramovich and his friends. Box number four has a controlled heating system for each seat. Andy said: "One day Abramovich came to us and said: 'my bottom is hot from the seat heating, but my head is cold'. It caught us a bit by surprise, since Abramovich comes from Russia, one of the coldest places in the world. So we told him: 'Roman, put a cap on', but he said (while Andy is imitating his heavy Russian accent): 'I am a billionaire, I do not do caps.' So we fixed a system to blow hot air on his head. Now he is hot in the head as well as his buttocks". The seats in the private boxes, such as that of Abramovich, cost a million pounds a season, whereas the agreement with a company interested in purchasing such a box is for a minimum of ten years, that is, ten million pounds.

The last attraction is sitting at 'The shed', the most known supporters' stand at Stamford Bridge. In the police capsule above us, several dozen police officers and thirty control screens broadcasting images from a hundred cameras at the same time. Forty unarmed police officers are in charge of the forty thousand people found in the stadium during the match. Four hundred security guards, wearing civilian clothes, not carrying weapons, are the only security force in the stadium.

Just before Andy bids us goodbye, he concludes: "I hope I managed to warm your heart a bit and turn you into Chelsea supporters".

Chelsea's history

After the tour, visitors are invited to be impressed by the history of Chelsea Football Club. The museum is big, much more than that of the Emirates Stadium in spite of the fact that Arsenal Football Club has won more titles in the history of English football. This indicates that the facts are not the only factors that influence the history of the football club. Exhibits in the Chelsea's museum are arranged chronologically, from the early twentieth century to present time. Photographs in black and white of supporters cheering their team, are spread on an entire wall at the entrance to the museum. Although it's possible to 'paint' pictures today by using a computer programme, they chose to show black and white pictures, leaving the visitor with a sense of tradition.

The club's history is introduced on about a 10 feet long fabric, from the ceiling to the floor. 'Chelsea was unique from the beginning' is written there. In 1904, Gus and Joe Mears purchased an Athletics stadium whose owners were in debt, and offered to turn it into a football club. The next fabric screen tells about the visit of King George V to one of the team's matches in 1920. By reminding this one-time guest appearance of the King in Stamford Bridge, royal support is granted to the group.

The large blue posters continue to tell the history of the club: their relegation to Division Two during 1924 followed by their comeback six years later.

The next poster tells about the 1939/40 season that was interrupted because of World War II. To maintain the morale of the armed forces and civilians, the government asked the football teams to go on playing. The black and white pictures show death and destruction, as expected from a World War.

In 1955, Chelsea won the English Championship for the first time in its history, and the club became one of the biggest in the country. The sixties and seventies were good decades for the blue team. They reached the FA Cup Final, to play in European match and even won a glorious 2–1 victory against Real Madrid.

In 1975 however, the club was relegated again to the second division. In the upcoming years Chelsea went up and down a league several times. All its assets were sold, and it faced bankruptcy. In 1982 it was sold to Ken Bates for the price of one pound sterling plus the covering of debts. A year later, it was nearly relegated to the third league then two years later, it finished first place in the league, and finally in 1984 it went back up to the first league.

The last poster in this museum is the one that will leave the supporter excited, enthusiastic and proud, just before leaving the room. It is called 'The Revolution'. Pictures of the club's heroes are shown with pride; Ruud Gullit, Roman Abramovich and Jose Mourinho. It says: 'investment in players started at a new level in 1995 with the signing of Ruud Gullit and Mark Hughes. Gullit became manager in 1996 and signed big stars'. In 1997 Chelsea won the FA Cup again and a year later, they took the League Cup and the UEFA Cup. In 1999, they qualified for the Champions

League and reached the quarter-finals. A year later they won the FA Cup and The Community Shield. In the summer of 2003 Roman Abramovich bought the club at a cost of sixty million pounds, and spent much more on bringing the players. In 2004, Jose Mourinho was brought to the club, whose picture on the poster is also the largest. Mourinho turned Chelsea to champions twice in a row, and changed the history of the club.

Just before ending the review of the club's history in the past century, a deep, determined voice turn to the supporters from the load speakers: "Get ready for the next decade!"

Public relations

Tours and museums at clubs are only one of the many means employed on a daily basis to praise the football club. Another, very important area that every football club needs to deal with in the era of rapid information and technology is working with the media.

"If you open the Sun newspaper, you will find at least two pages about Arsenal every week. This kind of publication cannot be bought with money", said Gabriel, one of the instructors at the club. The Public Relations Department is responsible for distributing messages to all types of media: print, broadcast and electronic as well as producing stories when there is not enough news to fill the entire pages. Before the English national team matches in the qualifying competition for Euro 2008, for example, the department invited journalists on a tour in the club's academy. The tour title was: 'This is how we train the next generation of English football'. Reports that were published following this tour marked Arsenal as the leading manufacturer of football players in the country. "Note, Capello," said one of them, "the future generation of the national team is raised in the Arsenal academy"

Along with the growth of the popularity of football, grew the need for a public relations department. The PR department doesn't only fuel existing media, but also acts as a media itself. It makes the club less dependent in other available media and works to improve the direct connection between the club and its supporters. Most football clubs in England today have several ways to communicate with their supporters; the most familiar ones are electronic mail and websites. The larger clubs often also publish their own magazines and produce their own TV channels as means to spread their stories around.

Clearly, all football clubs own an official website, which provides all the information that supporters in particular, football supporters in general and even journalists seek to find; it details match results, some necessary information before and after the matches, injury reports and Press Releases stories. Since the official website is the first and most reliable source of information, whoever is interested is use to opening it before any newspaper, TV station or other website. The media reports are also using information published on the website, so the public relations department is able to control the accurate timing and content that a specific detail of information is going to be published.

The club's website addresses a global audience. Among the rest, you can read the Arsenal's website in Chinese, Japanese and Korean. Chelsea website is available in the three languages as Arsenal, plus in Russian and Indonesian. For supporters who do not speak English the club's website becomes the main source of information. The clubs' public relations department provides all the knowledge and stories supporters worldwide want to read. This is how English football clubs become such strong international brands.

The costs of publication and translation of information in different languages is pretty high, but then again worldwide sales of club products compensate for it. The formula is simple: football clubs invest many resources in strengthening the ties with its supporters from all around the globe, thus the international supporters loyalty is strengthened. The expression of this loyalty is expressed by buying more of the club's products, so that eventually the expenses of the club on its website is not only insignificant, but is significantly negligible compared to the revenues. Arsenal's Web site had half a million hits every day during 2008.

Arsenal has a million supporters from around the world on its distribution list. Through the use of simple and cheap e-mail messages, the club sends updates to one million supporters almost on a daily basis. Once a week the supporters receive an online weekly newspaper that includes an after-match interview with the teams' manager – an interview that cannot be read anywhere else.

With half a million visits to the website each day, a distribution list of a million people who receive e-mail messages on a daily basis, and exclusive interviews and an online newspaper, the football club manages to avoid the need for its supporters to travel to other types of media. Moreover, the need to provide ongoing information requires journalists who follow the club to get information from its website and quote it. The clubs public relations department becomes a direct and indirect means of nourishing the connection with its supporters. This way, the club manages to do what was previously done by countries that had all means of media concentrated in their hands: to maintain and strengthen its force while engaging in-club political censorship. The effort the club invests in speaking in the native languages of its supporters is perceived as a kind gesture, making the supporters feel important, and a part of the community.

Success can be measured in financial terms; the new Emirates Stadium contains sixty thousand seats, most are sold to season ticket holders at the beginning of the season. In addition, forty thousand people are on the waiting list for a vacant seat in the stadium for many years now.

By using relatively simple means as an Internet website and a weekly e-mail, the football clubs in England make their supporters feel a part of an imagined community. And in order to be part of Arsenal's glorious football club community, you don't have to live in north London, not even in England. You don't even have to speak English.

The beginning of the end

A.

By the end of April the academies must inform the student whether it intend to retain or to terminate his registration. For those who graduated their training the answer will be a life changing one. Some of the players will be loaned to another club; one maybe two players will play for the first team of their club. These players have a long way ahead of them. They all will have to face challenges as well as temporary failures, as did David. Some will become successful, some less. They will have the support of the coaches in the academy through every step of the way.

The investment in the academies throughout the season, at the time of my visit, could not be measured only in financial aspects. Most of the job is done by education programmes and educational human resources. Money is necessary but it is no less important to know how to use it. The academies use money to reinforce their scouting network. But along them you can find academic staff consisting of trainers ranked 'Pro', the highest level, 'Guide 1' certified coaches, former professional football players, a physiotherapist, head of education and welfare, and teachers who are responsible for the educational aspect. The Children's training plan is complex and calculated, with every step they make being recorded, documented and retained as part of the overall training follow-up. Performance analysis of their skills in and off the pitch are conducted once a week together with the kids, once a month in the presence of a small team, and every six weeks with a large team in the presence of the player.

Whether the investment in academies is financial, professional, educational, emotional or any other type (either way each academy should set), its main goal in high quality training of the players growing in and out of it. When the target is set, it is much easier to find ways to achieve it. By the end of the 2007/08 season, not all of the clubs playing in the Premier League have come to realise the importance of academies. In an interview I conducted with one of the managers of one of the premier league's teams, I asked him about the club's academy. He could not tell me much. "I coach the first team. We have a loose relationship with the academy. It is not my job to know what is going on there". Three years later, after I returned to my hometown in Israel, I began hearing reports about important changes made in the management avenue of the academy by recruiting managers, coaches and professional teachers from all over England, and by expansion of the scouting team.

One of Arsenals academic successes during this season is the recovery and return of David to active play. David's team climbed above the red line, and three weeks before the end of the season, it was no longer in danger of being relegated. Just before David's loan period ended and his future was again on the table of Arsenal's Academy, he arrives to have dinner with Johnny's family for the last time. He sits with his back straight, his neck long, and his eyes are looking straight back at us while he admits: "Mission accomplished. I don't know where I'll be next season, but I am ready!" Two weeks later, I receive a phone call from Johnny happily telling me that David will be signed on a loan contract in the next season and will play with the great Tottenham. Even though David was not able to join Arsene Wenger's team, Tottenham Hotspur Football Club is a successful club, the holder of this season League Cup and the club's ambitions for the next seasons are high. David, who next year will be only nineteen, is happy and ready for the task. After he successfully crossed a difficult year he finally comes home, to north London, to Friday dinners and to Roy. Next year, a nice family with two parents, two children and a dog will live in a small neighbourhood in north London, meeting all statistical criteria of a bourgeois family. As north London residents, the family members are supporters of the Arsenal. Starting next season, another son will be added to the family. He plays with north London's rival club, Tottenham. When he does, Friday dinners will certainly be very interesting.

Farewell

The final game

The football season in England ends in May. The academies children go on a long summer vacation this weekend, which will continue until the start of next season. It is also the end of my research work in England. This Sunday will be the last time I'll take the train to Walthamstow central station and from there take a taxi to the Arsenal academy to see the children play.

This is a hot spring sunny day. Arsenal is the hosting Watford academy. Dozens of parents from both academies are standing on the sidelines; two grandparents, who are also Watford fans are sitting on two comfortable seats. They don't have any grandchildren playing at the academy, but as loyal fans, they escort the team's children wherever they go. Almost a year ago I met them uptown at their home ground; it was the same day Tom Ganot arrived to trial at academy. Their warm welcome helped me overcome the initial embarrassment, so they were first two fans I interviewed for my research.

Before the games begins, I meet Richard, one of the coaches at the academy. Everyone affectionately call him Richard Gere because when he speaks with the kids and their parents, he does it like a movie star. He is walking around between the pitches, wearing a short Arsenal shirt with a long sweatshirt hanging on his shoulders in a very stylish way. While walking, he throws encouraging comments to his players and some jokes to amuse their parents. Mr Smith, the director of the Academy, is standing on the sidelines at the moment, guiding his U16 young team toward another victory. The gaps between Arsenal's academy players and the Watford academy are quite large, and in less than fifteen minutes from kick-off it is already clear that the red wearing team is going to win this game. But as we already know, the result is not what matters. The process that these children went through throughout this season will remain with them for many years after the results will long be forgotten. I pass by the two pitches where children from the U10 teams are playing, six on six. Suddenly I realize how much they have grown in the past year; they still barely reach the height of the corner flag, but now they are stronger, more determined. This is their last game in the upcoming months; they do not want to go home without leaving a good impression on the coaches.

Cody and Ron are standing at the goals of the two pitches. Cody's father encourages him cheerfully. This time, Ron's father arrives; he doesn't say a word, only stands on the sidelines with a smile on his face. Cody seems disorientated at the goal, again, but somehow no ball manages to go passed him. It seems a bit like magic, as the Watford players often shoot at the goal. Ron, however, seems confident. As in the training from a few weeks ago, once again he steps out of the goal lines and calls his friends to go left, then right. And this time too, he takes balls out of the net. He doesn't lose his confidence. At one point, towards the end of the game, he kicks the ball straight at the feet of Watford's forward player and instantly pays for his mistake with another goal. In total, he takes in six goals. But he keeps his head high.

By the third quarter, Alex, one of Watford back players, could no longer breathe. Arsenal's strong attack exhausted him, and he can no longer run or deliver accurate balls. His parents stand on the sidelines; His mother is a young woman dressed in tight bright clothes, revealing her pregnant belly. His father is a lean man with a gentle face. You can see the concern for their son on their faces. Between cheering and trying to catch his look for a brief gesture of comfort, Alex's father needs to entertain Alex's little brother. He hugs his dad's feet, asking him to lift him to the sky. Alex's dad picks him up, turns him down and bring him to the grass, face down as if he was an airplane. The little one laughs his heart out. Both parents alternately trying to encourage Alex; one time his mother stands on the sidelines and calls: "Come on Alex, you are doing great". When Alex is too exhausted and no longer responds to her callings, they change strategy. She sits down on the grass, amusing the little brother, and Alex's father stands on the sidelines. "Come on Alex, come on". Alex does not have enough energy to even tie his shoelaces, which of course increases the chance of injury. When the ball goes out of play as a result of an Arsenal shootout just next to where Alex was standing, he looks at the ball as it travels away in despair. His father and I are looking at each other, smiling, and in silently agree to cooperate. I run to get the ball, and Alex" father holds his son, gets down on his knees and ties his laces tightly for him. The game is renewed. Alex, after the short rest, is able to run a little longer, but keeps falling behind. He keeps on trying to earn a few stolen moments of rest by stopping the flow of the game too often to tie his shoelaces. During one of these times, abandons the wing, and his team concedes a goal. "Come on Alex," his parents continued, "you're doing a great job". Alex looked at his parent's "You have to be kidding me, right?" But after the second and third time they repeated the same mantra, he gets up on his feet, and already manages to block the next attack.

The insistence of Alex's parents to continue encouraging him no matter what represents most of all the spirit of children's training and games in the academies. Starting from the ultimate objective of the Academy, which defines these games as friendly, fun-oriented games, to the support of their parents throughout their victories as well as their losses. This is the spirit that runs through the faithful spectators who come to watch the kids play and induce the pleasant atmosphere coaches like Richard create around their environment; It also runs through Cody's father whose uproarious laughter increases the spirit in the Arsenal Academy. And although Cody's father laughter is typical only for him, each academy probably has at least one 'Cody's father' of its own. All of these make the children feel they are capable and value. They are nice young lads.

Arsenal's academy declares that their primary objective is to 'make the kids enjoy the training and games in the academy'. It's a bit odd to place pleasure as a first goal, especially when it comes from a capitalist society that allegedly sees these children mainly as an economic investment. The financial goals of the academy are not a secret, they coexist with caring for the child. My day-to-day experience at the academies shows that both Arsenal and Chelsea's academies manage to achieve their financial goals as well as the moral ones. The children who come to practice and their families that come to watch and cheer them truly enjoy the time they spend there. This is achieved by rather simple means; a big lounge, a smiling staff, some sandwiches, soft and warm drinks at cost price, and a brief conversation between coaches and parents at every opportunity. Children and parents know to respect the opportunity given to them, and their attitude towards the academy's professional staff is fairly respectful. Understanding that everyone is here for the same purpose, which is primarily enjoyment and training of the young, creates a stress-free atmosphere. This way, weekly practices and Sunday games become an experience and a pleasant way to spend the weekend.

Towards twelve noon, when the games are about to end, a sense of sadness creeps into me. "Don't get attached to these kids", Aric once told me. "The chances you'll meet them when they become senior players are slim". That is maybe true, but to ask me not to get attached to these kids after such a long time, is like asking that tomorrow rain won't fall in England; chances are very low that it will happen. As a matter of fact, following the organisational changes made in the academies, chances are that in eight to ten years many more players will graduate the academies successfully than ever before. So I'm optimistic; especially when I look at Twinny, Marcus, and Ron. Twinny, as usual, is playing in a forward position, laughing and having fun on the pitch. He does not seem worried about anything. The balls are rolling over at him and he tries to shoot at goal or pass them to his friends. A ball that stayed still on the ground after Twinny tried to shoot it but kicked nothing but air, made him laugh to tears. After he kicks the ball for the second time, this time successfully, he is available to join his friends who are laughing with him. Marcus joins the laughing choir, revealing his two beautiful dimples. Marcus plays behind the striker, supplying Twinny with balls. In one of the attacks, he pushes forward from the right wing and hits a tremendous shot towards the left corner goalposts. Watford's 'keeper is standing still, shocked. The parents clap with excitement, and then take the time to comfort the 'keeper, "you couldn't do anything, son, could you?" Arsenal's U10 coach looks at the performance and smiles, he is satisfied. He is not worried about Twinny, Mark and all the rest of the players that he cultivated this year. He has no doubt that they will move on to the next stage in the academy, according to their age. For him this is a farewell; Next year he will get a new group of ten year olds, and teach them all the things he taught this group during this year. He did all he could do for them, and the result is wonderful, isn't it?

Ron is not as relaxed. His performance in this game was not good enough, not as was expected of him, and as he expected of himself. But that does not matter now; He continues running for every ball, pushing his team forward. The final whistle catches him with the ball in his hand, trying to initiate a final attack. His disappointment from the game can be seen in his small, innocence face. But I'm not worried; because despite the fact that Ron's performances are not always impressive, he always manages to lift himself after each goal he concedes, look up, and move on proudly and confidently as if nothing happened. This leads me to believe that one day I will see him again; he will then wear a football kit, with the number 1 on his back; and he will be proud, confident and self-assured, as he is today.

While the Arsenal players shake the referee hand, after they are done with the ritual handshake with all Watford players and their coach, and a second before they go down to the changing room, I say my goodbyes quietly. In recent months they have seen me, almost every week, standing on the sidelines of their training field. They heard me clapping them and chanting calls of comfort whenever they made mistakes. At first I was the 'lady with a notebook' and later on, 'the student from Israel'. They learned from their parents that I was writing a book about them, but were somewhat embarrassed to ask what for. It was forbidden of me to interview them for my research, and it is generally not a simple task to interview children so young. Still, after we shared so many hours of football, they as players, and me, as a supporter, I want to believe that my presence on the sidelines will be missed.

In spite of the embarrassment, I lean down to Ron's height and reach out my hand. "Good luck, son", I tell him, and place my hand on his blond hair. And so I say goodbye to the twins, to Cody, Jim, Alex, Chris and Marcus.

One day, maybe in ten years, I will see some of them on the TV screen while wearing the kit of a professional club in the Premier League. I will certainly be proud and happy that I had the privilege of seeing them successfully overcoming some of the obstacles in their training process, turning from children into the ideal figures of English football players. Meanwhile, farewell.

The carrot

An incentive

A familiar folk tale tells the story of a hard working farmer who wishes to reach from his house on the farm to the central market square in order to sell the fruits of his land, with the help of a single, old donkey. Day after day, the donkey walks on this hard path, down dirt roads, carrying a full load on his back. One day, the donkey was tired and refused to move on. He just stood there, with his feet planted in the ground. The farmer took the stick and hit the stubborn donkey's buttocks. The pain of the blow made him take a few more steps, and then he stopped again. The farmer gave him another hit and again, the donkey made a few more steps and stopped. So they moved on, each in his own way, all the way to the market and back. The next morning, the donkey, who got used to the beatings, stood in his place, stubborn than ever, refused to move. The farmer hit harder, until he almost injured the animal. Again, the donkey moved a few steps forward and stopped, until they reached the market. On the third day, the beatings were no longer useful, and the farmer was helpless.

He went on thinking what to do. He couldn't hit harder without the risk of killing the animal, which, of course is something that he didn't want to happen. Finally, a thought came in his head. He took a fishing line, attached a carrot to its end, and held it in a way that the carrot will always remain several steps ahead of the donkey. And the donkey, who deeply wanted a taste of the sweet vegetable, kept going and going until he reached the market square, without even feeling that he himself, did it.

Taylor report impact

While discussing the impact of the Taylor Committee Report on the disappearance of hooligan violence from football in England, the restrictions and penalties that are mentioned as a solution to deal with the problem are usually the main theme that comes up. And indeed, in the second and longer report published by the Committee it proposed a few steps to eradicate hooliganism from football stadiums. The first is the operation of closed-circle TV cameras supervising fans at all times during the game and setting up a national intelligence unit to locate potential violence (was also suggested by earlier committees). The second was to specify three actions as illegal. The actions are: throwing a missile, chanting obscene or racialist abuse and going on the pitch without a reasonable reason. Carrying out each of these actions would result in a criminal record in the police or a prosecution.

Referring to these recommendations only does not do justice to the vast, ambitious project of Lord Taylor. More that criticising the behaviour of fans at the football stadiums the Committee report also turns to examine large institutional bodies: the FL, the football clubs, the regional councils, the police and first aid services. Beyond the criticism that Lord Taylor has on the functioning (or it must be said – the lack of functioning) of these institutions in preventing the Hillsborough disaster, he has general criticism on their perception of the football game. "The atmosphere does not encourage pride in the ground or consideration for others", he writes, and adds: "A totally new approach across the whole field of football requires higher standards both in bricks and mortar and in human relationships". Taylors' Committee report severely criticises the reference to football fans as potential criminals. "There is force too in the view that if people are herded and confined as potential offenders, that concept may in some cases become self-fulfilling". When football fans are pre-treated as criminals, it is likely that they will also behave this way themselves.

Overall, the report suggested seventy-six sections to be treated. The four listed here directly affect the fans. About thirty sections bring detailed recommendations of the desired architecture of the stands and the overall football stadium, including: all seated accommodation, maximum capacities of terraces and the removal of fences. Two sections recommend the setup of new committees; one to advise the design of the stadium, the other to inspect and review all function specified.

Twelve sections detail the clubs' responsibility, fifteen detail the role of the police, and a dozen additional sections expend on the desired cooperation between parties responsible of providing first aid in the pitches.

The distribution of responsibilities in the report reinforces the ultimate goal of the Committee, which is, as mentioned in the report more than once: football fans arriving at the grounds, should enjoy a cultural and welcoming experience, they should receive proper compensation for the price they paid for the ticket. Treating them as cultural will also lead to such behaviour on their part.

The report's recommendations were accepted in England almost fully. It succeeded, in a fairly short time, to create a dramatic change in the behaviour of the fans. Taylors' Committee report did not seek to act directly on the hundreds of thousands of fans who come every weekend to watch football games. He turned to football clubs, the police and emergency services in the stadiums, and demanded that they change their way of action and their attitude toward the fans. As opposed to common perception, the violence did not disappear from the view of English football as a result of fear of fans from the firm hand of the police and the courts. Handling them in a proper manner as culture consumers coming to enjoy leisure time, will, in itself make them behave properly. Their good behaviour makes them feel an intoxicating all-English feeling of pride, as they are part of a Western civilisation. It flatters the national superego and designs them as the perfect model of supporters.

In the past year, prior to every home game at the Emirates Stadium, a short video clip is played on the big electronic screen. The video begins in a small bedroom of a young football fan. According to the speed of his body movements one can guess he is excited. He puts a red scarf around his neck, and rushes towards the door of his house. He will go to the stadium together with his father; they'll sit down in their seats. The suspense is conveyed to the viewer in an inspiring manner. Here they are eating something, having a cold drink. The cries of fans can be heard while the team's players are getting on the pitch. An opening whistle and the game begins. The kid's favourite team pushes forward to the goal. One particularly good attacks, bursts from the right wing. Pass ahead and..., all who are sitting in front of the boy stood up. The screen turns black, and only the soundtrack tells the story: joyful voices of celebrating fans. The young boy is looking at his father, you can feel he is disappointed. In a strangled voice he asks his father: "Did they score?" At that moment sixty thousand spectators at the Emirates Stadium are moved. The message could not be clearer, but it is written in white over black: "If you love football, sit down".

Arsenal fans love football, love their club, and as us all, they love to think of themselves as pleasant, caring and sensitive to others. So they sit for most of the game, giving everyone an equal chance to watch the game. They feel good, the football club looks great and English football looks good. There are those who would argue that this cultural transformation was achieved by manipulative means. One can certainly argue much about this question. For me, I want to believe that the change in the English football supporters' behaviour was not forced on them without they have nothing to say about it. This will underestimate the intelligence of hundreds of thousands of people. I believe that the change in behaviour implies the desire to take part in an advanced Western civilisation (without getting into the complex meanings of 'civilisation', 'Western' or 'advanced') and a genuine intent to reciprocate. During the seventies and eighties, English hooligan football supporters did not come to England's museums and cultural exhibits. Consequently, museums and cultural exhibits came to their local football pitch. And so, football their behaviour was changed for the best. Fear was not the cause for change. An overall aspiration for the good of all, was.

Returning home

My flight back to Israel is set for Tuesday, a week and a half after the end of the season. In ten days this period will end. There are so many people to say goodbye to. Only to Johnny I cannot say goodbye properly. A week after I told him I was leaving, he was already unavailable on the mobile phone. Roy is also not answering, and Johnny's mother, who answered the phone at his home, only said he was very busy. And how about Roy and David? "Everyone is fine, everyone's fine. So when you say you are leaving? Good luck in Israel, sweetie, OK?"

Saying goodbye to Johnny is also, to me, saying goodbye to England. This goodbye has a sense of sadness in it, but it is also optimistic. Just over a year ago, when I first arrived the country, without my suitcase, my cell phone charger or any idea about how to go on. I stood on the wrong side of the conveyor belt, and turned off the radio because I could not handle the intellectual challenge of listening to the fast flowing British accent; I forgot to take my clothes from the laundry; My knees were shaking with every step I took up the stairs to the second floor in the academies of Arsenal and Chelsea. Gradually, I learned to cope with my fear and embarrassment. I stood on the right side of the stairs, and stopped hiding behind clumsy suits. Over time, even listening to heated debates on the radio talking about the status of Steve McLaren in the English national team became simpler. Even plays I went to watch in the West End, the centre of cultural existence and the pride of London, have become clear from start to finish.

My behaviour changed during the past year. So, I remained seated throughout the football matches, just as the Emirates Stadium broadcast asked, and allowed the event planners entertain me in the stadium. The Football Association and the English football clubs actively ask individuals to behave properly. Some say they manipulate. I leave the moral judgment to the reader.

It is likely that people will have different opinions regarding the practices of the English football managers. Personally I think that as long as the main purpose of the English Football Association and its clubs is to benefit the supporters, to create a gentle football match, respectful and artistic, there is no harm in these actions. The common perception today is that the fear from the forces of the law, as it appeared during the reign of Margaret Thatcher, and the punishment which followed the Taylor Committee's conclusions, are the main cause for the dramatic change in English football after the nineties. If this perception was correct, however, an atmosphere of fear and reluctance of the law would dominate the football grounds today. This is not the experience I have seen in football grounds today, to say the least. At Stamford Bridge, for example, only forty policemen, unarmed, are placed in a sealed capsule located above one of the stands. Nonetheless, there are cameras that can identify each face out of the tens of thousands sitting there, in case of illegal activities. I believe that such actions are not carried out in the stands not out of fear of punishment, but simply because they are not proper. Just as if you will pay the train ticket to Cobham, even though you know that probably no one will check your ticket. Punishment, as even a peasant and donkey know, can be effective only up to a point. Then it ceases to hurt, and it is not possible to go on with the punishment policy without fear of completely crushing the branch. English football has also realised it. After implying a stricter punishment policy following the recommendation of the Taylor Committee report, which included long term bans from football grounds and arrest penalties for misbehaviour, they also started tying the carrot to the fishing-line. The carrot is expressed by the luxurious stadiums, by giving attention to the safety and enjoyment of the supporters in the matches, and finally by providing a sense of empowerment. Walking after a carrot has a much greater effect than any other stick could have.

During England national team matches in the new Wembley Stadium, while ninety thousand England supporters make their way to their seats, two huge signs saying 'We are England' welcome their arrival. The three lions crest stands proudly behind. The supporters get a feeling of self-importance. 'We are England!' Their feeling of belonging is bought at a relatively minor price of avoiding illegal activities such as violent behaviour and invading the pitch. English supporters usually will not consider getting on the pitch to celebrate the championship, not because their fear of punishment; it's just not the proper thing to do.

Still there are exceptions. Sometimes the supporters are too excited, forgetting the rules of behaviour for a moment, and doing what they normally wouldn't. At least on two occasions at the end of the 2007/08 season, for example, supporters invaded the pitch. One of those events occurred in a match between Leicester and Stoke City, Stoke supporters went down to the pitch to celebrate a win before the final whistle of the match. It could have been a serious story; headlines in large newspapers expressing shock, disgust, anger. But would it really help? After a few minutes of supporters' celebrations, which is defined as criminal offence, I remind you, a voice from the loudspeakers system asked Stoke supporters to clear the pitch so that the match can be completed. It took a few minutes, but at the end the supporters made their way back to the stands, and the match continues, without the intervention of the police, without a media fuss and without courts and penalties. Several thousand supporters invaded the pitch, without anything dramatic happening. Except for the fact that Stoke stayed another season in the league, of course.

Learning from others

There is no need to refer to everything that was done in England as a god-given truth. This book does not intend to idealise the political actions taken in England or demand that we bring it immediately and uncompromisingly to other societies around the world. I hope that this book was not called as a guiding book seeking to bring the west into what is the alleged Orient. There might be behaviours that do not fit or are not appropriate for everyone. I will add, while I am at it, that I do not see learning from other cultures admission of failure of another culture. An educated person learns from the mistakes of others, and England, over the years have made many mistakes through which one can learn lessons that could be applied. Implementation of football as a cultural event in many places will not succeed unless we learn carefully about all the means that were used in England and we cease believing that imposing fear and terror on supporters is a legitimate and correct way to prevent violence. This conclusion is correct not only in football. There are many more areas in which you can make use of the conclusions presented here, in the fight against car accidents or in the fight against bulling in schools. If we convince those who hold the wheel that driving is actually pleasant and that courteous behaviour could makes them become better people, maybe we can bring about a significant change. After all, most people want to be good. The carrot is a continuous and therefore more effective means than the stick, which is thrown inconsistently. These goals may be too big, but remember that only twenty years ago people did not believe it would be possible to beat the hooliganism problem.

The picture painted here represents my opinion. This is my experience and my impressions from the time spent in England. This is my impressionist painting. I believe other people have their own impressionist paintings, which are equally legitimate, of course. A variety of opinions are important for creating a fruitful discussion. If I could inspire such a discussion, I paid my dues. As an anthropologist, that's all I can ask.

Epilogue

In the morning of May nineteenth, I am all packed and ready, waiting for the taxi driver to take me to the airport. In two more days Chelsea and Manchester United will play in the Final of the Champions League. I will watch this match from Israel. I dial to Israel from the taxi. Zero, zero, nine, seven, two, eight, six... after one ring my mother answers. You can hear in her voice that she is excited. "See you tomorrow morning". For the first time in months, we say goodbye only to meet again in a few hours. My cell phone is quiet for the rest of the way. Almost all the farewells have been made. Future meetings were set. At five o'clock in the evening, local time, I go to the check-in position. A last look at the English bureaucracy makes me smile. The relaxed atmosphere calmed my fear of airports. Just before I leave my heavy load with the friendly attendant and enter the departures gate, I recognise a familiar face. Two feet are running, short of breath, wearing an outfit of a café employee in Piccadilly' square. Johnny.

More than a year has passed since I first saw Johnny's face. It was late at night, I was so scared and frightened, and Johnny, wearing his pyjamas outside an apartment building in Victoria Street, was the most relaxing and cheerful thing I could have thought of; and now, thirteen months later, more at ease this time, I am so much happier to see Johnny approaches to say goodbye.

A group of people is lagging behind Johnny. His mother and father, Roy and David, close than ever. They all came to say goodbye.

"I have been calling for a week", I tell Johnny in my excited voice. "You weren't available".

"We wanted to surprise you, all of us", Johnny explains.

His mother adds: "I was so close to telling you, you must forgive me for that brief phone call. I don't know how to keep secrets, and I was really close to ruining the surprise".

"Well well, as long as everything worked out for the best", Johnny's father continues with his typical pragmatism.

"You know that in forty-eight hours Chelsea and Manchester United will face the Champions League Final. It is an historical event, isn't it?" Johnny and Roy's mother did not abandon her role as information provider of the group.

"Where are you planning to watch the match?" I ask. Roy and David, once again close and happy, as if the hard year behind them almost never happened, say: "We planned to watch it together at the pub next to our house. I wish you could come..."

Only Johnny, who already caught his breath, doesn't say anything. Pictures of the players from both teams are aired on TV screens above the exit gate. John Terry and Frank Lampard are training for the historic match, taking place in two days. Alex Ferguson's answers from the press conference are on replay over and over again, causing Johnny's silence to sound louder. When we hug one last time, right next to the exit gate, I allow myself for the first time to cross the borders of the local restraints, and allow a few stubborn tears to fall. When the hug is released, I look at Johnny's eyes for the last time, I think I know exactly what he thinks; as with all significant moments in his life, Johnny thought that you could make a great movie out of this moment, even if he knows that movies ending with airport goodbyes are already completely corny.

Acknowledgments

During the years 2007/08 I lived and did fieldwork in London. My fieldwork included visiting football academies, watching football matches, interviewing managers, football coaches, supporters and parents, reading newspapers, websites, governmental reports, books and almost all there is to read about English football. I am grateful for all the help I have received from the people in charge. It was the most significant experience of my professional life.

During that period of time I was lucky to have my family and friends from Israel visit me a lot. One of the most common phrases I have heard from my visitors was "I should have been born British", said with a very nostalgic tone. That comment meant to say that they believe that the British norms and conduct are much more appropriate to the speaker, especially if you compare them to the norms and conduct that are usually associated with the Mediterranean state of Israel. My mother did not visit me while I lived in England. Actually, excluding a two days visit during a fourteen countries in fourteen days organised tour, my mother did not spend any real leisure time in England. She did not watch a musical or has ever been to a football match. But of all those people that came to visit me, for me, she was much more English-like, as I know England.

My mother was the most forgiving person I ever knew. She never cared for the ethnic origin/race/gender of the other person and always spoke in defence of the underdog. She believed that love and understanding can solve all the problems of the universe and always preferred the use of a carrot over the use of a stick. Only now, six months after she passed away, I think I know why I was so inspired by England and by English football. The practices of peace making been that have been used since the end of the last century reminded me of her. I deeply regret the fact that she did not live to see this book come out in English.

I am in debt to many for the publican of this book. For the Hebrew version published in 2010 I thank the department of Sociology and Anthropology at Ben Gurion University of the Negev, Resis Nehara publication house, Avi Meller, Nimrod Lass, Viko Hadad, Amnon Raz and the one and only Arik Yahalomi.

For the English version I want to thank Liya Dahan and Yael Avivi. Special thanks to Steve Caron and DB Publishing for believing in this book. An Israeli student writing a book about English football can easily be viewed as a person trying to sell ice to the Eskimos.

Last but not least, my love and admiration to my family for putting out with my obsessions. To my father Shalom, my parents in law Amnon and Edna, my brothers and sisters Itzik, Eli, Diana, Naama, Talia, Doron, and their children. And to Ran, Lilly and Emmie – you are the reason for it all.

ND - #0219 - 270225 - C0 - 234/156/7 - PB - 9781780915319 - Gloss Lamination